TESTIMONIES AND REFLECTIONS

Books by Herbert Mason

Memoir of a Friend: Louis Massignon
A Legend of Alexander and The Merchant and the Parrot, dramatic
    poems
The Death of al-Hallaj, a dramatic narrative
Gilgamesh, a verse narrative
Summer Light, a novel
Moments in Passage, a memoir
The Passion of al-Hallaj by Louis Massignon, 4 vols. (translator)
Two Statesmen of Mediaeval Islam, a study
Reflections on the Middle East Crisis (editor)

LOUIS MASSIGNON (1883–1962)

Testimonies and Reflections

ESSAYS OF LOUIS MASSIGNON

Selected and introduced by
HERBERT MASON

University of Notre Dame Press
Notre Dame, Indiana

Copyright © 1989 by
Herbert Mason
All Rights Reserved
Manufactured in the
United States of America

Library of Congress Cataloging-in-Publication Data

Massignon, Louis, 1883–1962.
  Testimonies and reflections.

  Translated from the French.
  1. Islam. 2. Sufism. I. Mason, Herbert, 1932–
II. Title.
BP49.5.M3A25 1989   297   88-40327
ISBN 0-268-01733-6

To James Langford
with affection and deep respect

Contents

x CONTENTS

Acknowledgments

All of the essays included here were drawn from two collections: Louis Massignon, *Opera Minora*, 3 vols., ed. Y. Moubarac (Beirut, 1962–63); Louis Massignon, *Parole donnée*, ed. V. Monteil (Paris, 1962). Three of the essays were translated previously from papers given by the author at the Eranos Conferences, Ascona, Switzerland, and published by Princeton University Press: "The Idea of the Spirit in Islam," "Nature in Islamic Thought," and "Time in Islamic Thought," trans. Ralph Manheim, *Eranos Yearbooks*, vols. 3 (1957) and 6 (1968). "The Notion of 'Real Elite' in Sociology and in History" appeared in *The History of Religions, Essays in Methodology* (University of Chicago Press, 1959), edited by Mircea Eliade and J. M. Kitagawa. Three essays were written originally in English by Louis Massignon: "Gandhian Outlook and Techniques," "The Transfer of Suffering through Compassion," and "Meditation of a Passerby on His Visit to the Sacred Woods of Ise." The remaining twelve essays were translated specifically for this volume: "Salman Pak and the Spiritual Beginnings of Iranian Islam" by Katherine O'Brien; "The Three Prayers of Abraham" by Allan Cutler; and the others by the editor with special assistance from Danielle Chouet-Bertola. The final manuscript was typed by Edna Newmark. The copy editor was Ann Rice. The volume was made possible through the continuing interest and generous support of Prince Sadruddin Aga Khan and Mr. Paul Mellon.

Introduction

Louis Massignon (1883–1962) was one of France's leading students of the Islamic world. He was a distinguished professor of that most privileged of French academic institutions, the Collège de France, founder of the Institut des Études Islamiques, and director of studies at the École Pratique des Hautes Études in the religious sciences section. In addition to being for a time professor of Arabic at the new Egyptian University of Cairo, he was founder and guiding spirit of numerous journals and groups of scholarly researchers. His contribution to the field of Islamic studies was enormous and continues to be felt through the work of his many students in Europe, America, and the Muslim countries. His membership in all the major foreign academies of science attested to his achievements during his lifetime.

He also had a distinguished military and diplomatic career, highlighted by frontline service as an infantry officer in World War I, by his work with T. E. Lawrence on the Sykes-Picot Commission for Palestine, and by his wide-ranging contacts as French Cultural Ambassador to the Near East.

A tireless traveler, he was also a husband, father, a Catholic convert regarded, on the contrary, as a convert to Islam by many Muslim friends and colleagues, a Franciscan tertiary, and, finally, a Catholic priest of the Melkite Rite.

This terse sketch of his life is intended only to indicate what he himself referred to as points along his "courbe de vie." In fact, some imposition of form and order on his varied and sometimes perplexing life is both necessary and impossible to achieve. Once one comes to know him, his themes, idiom, tone, and points of reference and view, one suspects the key to understanding him is acceptance of the paradox of his complete candor and his elusiveness. He is the least simple to portray of his distinguished contemporaries among scholars, writers, statesmen, soldiers, and religious; yet for all his complexity or because of it he was the one most in awe of simplicity and most identified by others with such kindred words as sincerity, friendship, devotion, and fidelity.

As a student of the Islamic world, the subject on which he made his major scholarly contributions, he was trained as an orientalist, that is, in a methodology associated with the development of European colonialism and hegemony over (in the French instance that concerns us here) the Near East and North Africa. Orientalism is a training that nowadays is dying out in Europe but is practiced admirably by scholars among former colonized peoples trained by Europeans. It is barely known in its purest form in the American hemisphere save among a few students trained abroad decades ago.

Orientalism in its (dare one say *Faustian*) European form was both a romantic impulse and a scholarly state of mind involving a mode of inquiry that was presumptive, indeed often arrogant, amoral, and acquisitive, highly technical, and exhaustively authoritative. The great masters of classical orientalism of the German, French, and British schools, with individual luminaries scattered about within Dutch, Italian, and Spanish scholarship, were distinguished and forbidding gentlemen indeed; and the results of their researches were in many instances monumental if inaccessible to the general reader. On all but one level they were the equivalents of great master musicians and ballet choreographers. Unfortunately the one level was the crucial one of communication.

Louis Massignon, unlike most of his predecessors and contemporaries, had a rare blend of meticulous training and an ear for the music in his own and in another culture's soul. Orientalism, as he animated it, was both an adventure and an imaginative investigation. Its initial amateur spirit gave way only grudgingly in him to professional pedanticism and was saved ultimately from it by religious transformation and awe. The linguistic tools necessary for serious study were his at an early age; and being armed with familial, cultural, and financial support, travel and adventure were virtually predestined.

While genius (a word associated with him when young) had its own predictability, spiritual and moral understanding was elusive and uncertain of attainment and among many otherwise intelligent minds was regarded as of sentimental value only. Undoubtedly Massignon shared the latter view until his dramatic experience of May 1908 in Iraq, an experience recalled vividly by him in the essays of the present volume, and one that led to his conversion. All of his writing, teaching, speaking, and personal relationships subsequent to that "axial event," as he called it, were energized by an inner passion both to know and to understand and were guided by an extraordinary self-discipline and sensitivity to the spiritual dimension of things. Little of his personal eloquence, however, was captured in his major written contributions to French orientalism, including his rigorous collection and analysis of primary Islamic written and oral sources of historical, sociological, and religious documentation. Only in his public lectures, correspondence, and personal encounters was his eloquence heard at large, until, that is, he began to write late in his life articles and essays of engagement in current affairs, notably the Algerian War, in which he recalled vividly his earlier experiences and became for the French public a figure of political controversy and even scandal.

This is not to say that his magnum opus *The Passion of al-Hallāj* in its 1922 two-volume edition wasn't profoundly eloquent and an expression of his unique fusion of science and lyricism. But these qualities were made accessible to a wider audience only when his own life became radicalized politically and religiously in the 1940s through his growing interest in the person and teaching of Gandhi and his deepening awareness during the same period of the needs and aspirations of France's colonies of Algeria and Morocco. Persons who knew Massignon through his scientific or diplomatic work regarded him with awe but also as truly French and thoroughly establishment. Those who knew him as a Gandhian, a street demon-

strator against the war in Algeria, and a rather strangely voca-
tioned Melkite priest, considered him bizarre, confounding, and
troublesome. The "two Massignons" were unified all along, however, by a conversion "shock" that left him with an unshakeable
sense of the active presence of the Transcendent One Who called
one to justice, to truth, and to compassion. He expressed this
calling in many nonpublicized ways, including his years of visiting prisons and teaching fundamental skills to prisoners in prepa-
ration for their rehabilitation. When he took to the streets in
the late 1950s to witness for justice and peace between French
and Algerians he was echoing not merely Gandhi but al-Hallāj,
who had given his life for justice and peace in the Baghdad of
922 A.D. and who was the subject and friend of Massignon's
life work, begun with conviction in May 1908. And when in
October 1961 he and a group of his spiritual friends scrambled
down a bank of the Seine to try to pull ashore the bodies of
Algerians shot and thrown into the river by French police, he
was raising "the cry of Antigone," as *Le Monde* expressed it in
its October 18 issue, out of his long understanding of war and
its victims.

The unique quality of Massignon, which became more apparent as he grew older, was not his far-ranging intellect and
its ability to find and read texts that eluded others' notice, but
his exceptional piety, something often associated with deeply
intelligent people but not usually with intellectuals. And he
was definitely an intellectual; he just didn't make an idol of his
mind. The essays of this volume were selected purposely to high-
light his own expression of this rare combination of intellect
and piety. Two volumes recently published in Paris (*Presence
de Louis Massignon, Hommages et Témoignages* and *L'Hospi-
talité Sacrée,* both 1987) particularly evoke this combination
through personal memoirs by forty-five persons who knew him
and through selected letters from his vast correspondence. In
terms of the public at large, the long-range implications of his
personal testimonies and reflections as a Catholic and as an
Islamist are only beginning to be considered.

It will soon be evident to the reader that the essays of this volume are not those of a detached historian, which he could indeed be, but of a man involved in history and at times of a history maker; a "witness." One of Massignon's early models of cultural crossover was Sir Mark Sykes, whom he honored in a memorial on April 21, 1919, and which could just as easily have been said of him (*Opera Minora*, III, p. 418):

> It was neither a financial scheme for economical prospection, nor an adventurous wish for unilateral expansion, which led him on. It was the maturing of a wide personal experience, and the free will of a deep love which moved him towards his friends of these Eastern nationalities. . . . He had visited all their towns, crossed their wilderness, and climbed their mountains, several times; he was truly fond of them, and knowing him, they all confided in him. Not only had he studied the present conditions of their social life, drawn powerfully in his books, he had also an extensive and exquisite knowledge of their history.

By the late 1940s the last hints of any colonial fondness were gone from Massignon himself and what remained were his deep friendships and an array of his own distinguished books.

The last eight years of Massignon's life were devoted to writing, speaking, and demonstrating against the Algerian War. All else seemed to take a secondary position in his thoughts, including the completion of his much expanded second edition of *The Passion of al-Hallāj*. The last twelve years he was a Melkite priest, offering the sacrifice daily in a chapel built in his home. Family and friends supported him closely throughout and were undoubtedly partly responsible for energizing and sustaining him in those years of crisis for two peoples he dearly loved.

In the end, he believed that only the *qibla* (the orientation point) of God, the personal Creator and Redeemer, was a true and efficacious orienting point for one's rescue from oneself and for civilization's from itself; and the mystics of Christianity and Islam especially were for him the guides to this rescue and elevation whose testimonies he had collected assiduously and faithfully from their primary sources throughout his life.

A few words must be said on the division of this collection into three "parts." The division is arbitrary and the selection is eclectic. The connecting theme is simply the title itself, *Testimonies and Reflections.*

The essays in Part One express in various ways Louis Massignon's early experience and notion of "witnessing," of friendship, of transcultural understanding, of mystical authenticity, of engagement in history. Their pace as a group is intense, their tone at times irascible.

Part Two consists entirely of essays in his Arabist-Islamist mode and as such is more deliberately scholarly and in some instances highly technical, while in fact extending the themes and allusions of Part One. These essays have been stripped for the general reader of most of their scholarly apparatus, including diacritical marks and copious footnotes.

Part Three might indeed be called "dialogue with civilizations," to borrow a heading from one of the French collections. It conveys with high immediacy, I believe, the tone of a resolved yet ever curious "witness" in his own right.

Many of the selections were delivered as talks, a few in charged circumstances. All were composed or "sketched out" (his particular stylistic bent) by a man in his mid-fifties or older who had already completed twelve major books in his proper field of Islamic studies and who was now composing in his minor, if more personal, key. Most were the reflections of a man over sixty-five who was becoming an actor in history and, to many who would survive him, a legend. He had lost none of his power to engage, to confront in disturbing ways, and to recall an astonishing array of historical knowledge in correspondence with almost any occasion. The essays show glimpses of mystical knowledge in lyric flight and always a deep compassion for humankind.

While the translations can at best only approximate the mind and energy of their author, it is hoped they will point readers to the originals and, as he would say, beyond them to their primary sources.

PART ONE

The Three Prayers of Abraham
(1949)

Patriarchae nostri Abrahae omnium credentium Patri (October 9, Roman Martyrology)

Among the men of prayer and spiritual longing who have appeared on the threshold of this generation, three have left a testimony of God's Holy Name, an incorruptible trust, a spiritual vow, for those to whom they spoke of Him, to be passed on to coming generations in order that they, in turn, might experience its saving power. J. K. Huysmans, Léon Bloy, and Charles de Foucauld — all three of them, in their return to God, were characterized by a discipline of fasting and prayer that was among the starkest and harshest that the Latin West has known, and also the closest to the great immemorial asceticism of the East. I refer to the discipline of La Trappe, which was the daughter of St. Benedict through St. Bernard and Rancé and the granddaughter through St. Benedict and St. Augustine of St. Basil and St. Pacomius. In the face of the growing social depravity and the mystery of iniquity of our own times, the Trappist discipline is humanity's ultimate recourse. It is significant that in carrying the entire ascetic tradition of India and the Far East out to its logical conclusion by rescuing it from the egotistical solipsism of the yogis in order to transform it into a discipline of healing expiation capable, as we have seen, of surpassing the means of action employed by colonialism, an idolatry of gold and of blood, Gandhi, in a powerful death on behalf of the poor and the persecuted, overtook the effort of the Slavic hermit saints, spiritual descendants of St. Pacomius and St. Basil, whose last echo Tolstoi transmitted with the love of the evangelical

Beatitudes. Asceticism is not a private luxury preparing us for God, but is rather the profoundest work of mercy, which heals broken hearts by offering up instead its own broken bones and wounded flesh.

Almost fifty years ago, while praying and attempting to imitate these three friends and elders [Huysmans, Bloy, and Foucauld] in a secluded place in the desert of Upper Egypt, Fao, where once stood Phboou, Pacomius's hermitage, the first historic center of militant Christian asceticism, I was permitted to taste its force when the determined ignorance of a companion who had been dragged along to that point was suddenly released for an instant by an infusion of divine grace. There, in the desert of the Forty Days, our vow to join battle, the final battle, for the salvation of humanity, took shape, through fasting and prayer. The desert is silence and terror. Fasting is, above all, the silencing of the voices of the flesh, and prayer is the daughter of the fear of both the Judgment and the Judge. Speech is perceived in silence. God's gift informs prayer. In the Arabian desert, man understands the still abandon of the innocent gecko lizard and the cruel hooded falcon in the master's hand which comes to rest upon them. In the Iranian steppe, driven at night between automobile headlights which track it down, the gazelle falls to its knees to weep. Do we understand the divine necessity which forces us to silence and to prayer? It is the call wherein God offers the two supreme weapons which He paternally offered to the Son in order to enter into his public Passion; and these weapons are forged only among the anchorites and hermits of the Carmelite, Cistercian, and Trappist Orders, whether they like it or not. When the objection was voiced to Foucauld that he had left the Trappist monastery, he, breaking his bonds, affirmed that if the Word left the silent cloister of eternity at the request of the silent Mary, It returned to that cloister with the Ascension, breaking silence between these two dates only at the urging of love.

The call of the church militant is first expatriation and then election of the homeland. It is not good for everyone to reside in the same place all his earthly life (St. Bernard himself was not permitted to observe his Rule fully, which stressed that the monk should stay within the cloister). What is essential is to have made a retreat with sufficient seriousness in order to preserve throughout one's life the living mark and the exemplary imprint of the Rule, the guiding orientation, in order to transmit it to others to come. Huysmans passed through Igny, Bloy through Soligny, while Foucauld himself left Cheikhle (which is now deserted, its last Trappist, Father Philippe, was nailed to the door, like an owl, by Kurdish brigands in 1915). But there they were mobilized for the supreme "Holy War," the *jihad akbar* of the Arabs. They only left their cloisters in order to offer a testimony on behalf of justice for the souls of those living outside. Their testimony, whose furious expansion has not yet been choked off by the "societies of friends" who work to dull its effects by exploiting it in a fashion which offers so little reward, arises out of the Cistercian Order and its very efficacy is bound up with the preserving of the original purity of the Trappists. When the monasteries of the strict observance become weak, as was seen in France before 1789 and in Russia before 1917, society begins to collapse.

These three cited witnesses are counted as laity (Foucauld became a priest only at age forty-three and as such remained secular and alone). Such is the way. Certainly, it would be desirable in these days of social action to be able to rely upon the public testimonies of communities constituted and consecrated for this purpose. But it is precisely the abuse of their privileges which fossilizes them and deprives us of their help. A testimony is worth something only when it is personal, committing a name that is ordinarily unknown during the man's lifetime. Bloy and Foucauld experienced something of this; and though Huysmans knew such notoriety late in life, it came when he was already terminally ill with cancer.

When God chooses a witness, even in the humblest domain, He makes that witness unrecognizable and hateful to others. He veils his soul in order to defend it against vainglory, just like the Touaregs veil themselves against the sandstorm, in order that the soul may expose its face only to Him. But at the same time this disguise enables the witness to substitute for others in order, unbeknown to them, to bear their sins and to deflect from them their punishment. Despite the growing toxicity of the poisons of atheistic technology, all God needs to disinfect our wounds are homeopathic doses of holiness. But He must find it. *Salutem ex inimicis.* He takes such doses from among those to whom persistence has given the bitter meaning of sin. He extracts them, one by one, from their depths of sorrow, and throws them alone to the world-at-large.

How? He calls them with friendly voices, the voices of the "apotropaic" witnesses who succeed one another from generation to generation (this was one of the strongest certainties of Huysmans and these are what the Arabic tradition calls the *abdal*, the "apotropaics," the heirs of Abraham, endowed, often unbeknown to themselves, with his power of intercession, of healing compassion), in order to lead them to the threshold of that narrow gate, which is difficult enough to see and almost impossible to pass through, leading into the homeland, the land of promise.

At that moment when the terror which conceals from us the approach of our final end makes us turn inwards, to return to our origins, when the toxic malice of our disagreements forces us to seek out once again our common ancestors, it is wise to take up once again the links in the spiritual chain of pure witnesses upon which we depend (the *series episcoporum* of Christian ordinations, the *asanid* of the Muslim tradition), and which lead us back to Abraham all the more boldly the more desperate our situation. More than any other defender of lost causes, Abraham is an intercessor. For the other saints who can cure us of despair merely cauterize our transitory wounds whereas Abraham continues to be invoked as their Father by twelve million circumcized Jews, who aspire to take possession for themselves alone of that Holy Land which was long ago promised to him, and by four hundred million Muslims who trust patiently in his God through the practice of their five daily prayers, their betrothals, their funerals, and their pilgrimage. The Jews have no more than a hope, but it is Abrahamic. The Muslims have no more than a faith, but it is Abraham's faith in the justice of God (beyond all human illusions). And these two centuries-old declarations, as immobile as once-active volcanoes, hang over the unfolding of the transitory joys and cares of the uncircumcized in the twilight of their idols. Except that in searching thoroughly we find, scattered everywhere, the still warm cinders of a tremendous eruption, still Abrahamic—that of the accursed city which was excluded by God because of its self-love, which concentrated all of its faith and hope in a pact between men in the manner of convicts; a pact, nevertheless, which once bound them to Abraham and which, twice, forced Abraham to pray for them even though they were the most forsaken of the creatures of God; a pact of the loyalty of convicts, which for Abraham was the surprising point of departure for his ecumenical vocation. A word given, respected, the last refuge of divine transcendence, of the faithful testimony which quickens all faith and all hope.

Of the three solemn prayers of Abraham, before the prayer for Ishmael, the Arab and the Muslims, before the prayer for Isaac and the Twelve Tribes descended from his son Jacob, the first prayer which we must take up once again is the prayer for Sodom, without either unhealthy curiosity or hypocritical disdain, in the evening Angelus, *"che volge il disio"* (Dante, *Purgatorio* 8:1).

This is not the place to examine the conditions under which the texts of these three prayers have been handed down to us through all of the mishaps to which the copyists and translators have been exposed. The discoveries of Semitic archaeology are bringing us closer and closer to a continuity in the steps which "external" history had to traverse in order to overtake the Abrahamic milieu and emphasize more and more the exceptional character and monolithic permanence of the two circumcized groups, the Jews and the Arabs, in the face of the Christian apostolate. As for any child who wants to understand his father, a hiatus faces us the uncircumcized, which can only be bridged by a theological faith (or a hope or a love of equal force), because God is truly the Father. Here is where the spiritual chain of witnesses intervenes, corroborating the transmission of the sacramental powers, *salva inerrantia.*

Like history, the geography of today brings us closer to Abraham by focussing our attention on a high place of humanity which began with his own. There still is the Muslim Arab, with his double *qibla* (the focal point of prayer toward Mecca and Jerusalem) and the Passover celebrating Jew, for whom "next year in Jerusalem" is becoming "today." Here is the physical return of the two inimical brothers to the chosen places of their resurrection (the al-Aqsa mosque for the Muslims, the Temple for the Jews, only 150 meters apart on the same *Haram*); and only 350 meters from the Anastasis or Qiyama (the Holy Sepulcher) of the Christians, who, because they have not yet developed sufficient consciousness of their "Abrahamic adoption," are not yet concerned about returning to Jerusalem to await the Parousia of the Lord. Nevertheless, there in Jerusalem the Christians have Arab witnesses of their faith and the geographical convergence of the pilgrims of the three Abrahamic faiths in one and the same Holy Land, trying to find there that justice which Abraham through his threefold trial found in his God, led a year ago to a horrible war. Why? Because the Christians have not yet fulfilled their complete responsibility toward their brothers in Abraham. Because they have not yet explained to them how to love that Holy Land which is one of the two terms of the promise to Abraham. Desire for the Holy Land could not be entirely "theological" because God is not "mother." But as Christians, who can call Abraham our Father only by adoption and a "pact of alliance," who thereby are substitutes for his allies of the Pentapolis (the future Dead Sea) whom Abraham saved the first time with 318 troops (cf. Gideon, etc.), but could not save the second time, we think that the Holy Land ought to be for humanity the symbol of a "kindergarten," of a "human nest" prepared for our flight toward the bosom of Abraham, of a pure maternity, to which we must "return," at least by meditation, if we want to be reborn in the Spirit, as Christ said to Nicodemus. Let the Christians, meditating with Huysmans and Bloy on the desire for the hyperdulia, which about a century ago, was born within the Western Church with the French pilgrimages to the sites of Mary's apparition, understand that her true home is Nazareth where, as Foucauld has shown us, she makes us find, with her, the "fiat" of the vocation. Let them also think about their substitutes of the time of Abraham, about his allies of the accursed Pentapolis, about our lost brothers "down there," for whom Huysmans prayed, I know, during his final agony. For them, it is not a question of joining together in any pilgrimage, even only a mental one, because not wanting to find God as a third in their friendship of two, they can only be cured in isolation. But once isolated, in harsh retreat, it is possible to show them, in the depth of their spiritual sterility, the Nazarean Virginity in order that they may love with an admiring love as pure as that of the Christian for the Cross: the Virgin, the supreme symbol of the transcendent deity (*al-mathal al-a'la*, in Islam). For that admiration, that fertile adoration, is the reason why God allowed Sodom to exist.

The first prayer of Abraham is the prayer which he uttered on behalf of Sodom to the Philoxenia at Mamre in a veritable theophany. There "that man of all beginnings" and all endings was caught between the two substantial words of his union with God: *"Lech l'cha"* (= "go out": of Ur) and *"Hineni"* (= "here I am": I am ready to go to Mt. Moriah). He had abandoned the townsman's life of Chaldea to take up the life of a wandering shepherd. He planted the first stake which rooted him in the Promised Land very near his own future tomb. The perfect hospitality which he offered to his three mysterious visitors (*"tres vidit et Unum adoravit"*), who came to overwhelm him with the promise of Isaac, led them to test him: Is Abraham, now that he is assured an heir, going to continue to look after the people of Sodom, allies of his nephew Lot, whom he had already saved once by force of arms, or will he disavow his pact of fidelity with them when he learns that they have gone astray by their iniquity? Then the angels told him that the people of Sodom had committed terrible sins and that the Lord was going to de-

stroy them. But Abraham himself had come into this land as a
stranger, a *ger:* a guest; and they were his guests. The guest is
sacred and still remains so, and Abraham entered into that extraordinary debate with God, that sublime haggling over numbers which upset Bloy. Abraham could no longer summon 318
troops to rescue them, but it was from among the people of
Sodom themselves that he strove to discover, in the divine pre-
science which questioned him, their deliverers, for which he
made up a prayer which became ever more pure, capable of raising up within Sodom fifty, forty-five, forty, thirty, twenty or
only ten righteous men, so that it might be saved. God accepted
Abraham's proposal but only three righteous men could be found
in the city (and among them St. Lot of Segor, as the Crusaders
called him) and four of the five cities of Sodom were burnt to
the ground. But just as the requirement that Abraham offer up
a sacrifice remained unfulfilled, after Isaac's deliverance, until
the sacrifice at Calvary, so also the promise of the ten righteous
men remains unfulfilled and it is necessary to remind God of
it in the name of Abraham, to remind God of what that uprooted promise cost Abraham—first, Ishmael's exile, driven out
into the desert with Hagar by Sarah, then the offering up of
Isaac upon the altar unbeknown to his mother Sarah: two cruel
tests of love caught up and deeply involved in the extreme ve-
hemence of his compassion praying for Sodom, tokens of his
blessing for the uncircumcized.

Sodom is the city of self-love which objects to the visitation
of angels, of guests, of strangers, or wishes to abuse them. It
is the city of guilds, of intellectual circles, whose recruitment
proceeds not by familial genealogy but by technical initiation,
by a very quickly confining "paedagogia," as H. Marrou has
noted with regard to education in the Greek city states, in a
"paederastia." It is based on the distinction between the market-
place and the home, between masculine freedom and feminine
modesty in behavior. The social legacy of civilization requires
that men have a genuine affiliation, confining them within a
vow of celibacy that does not necessarily imply any chastity,

as, alas, can be seen among too many physicians and musicians. Similarly, domestic culture and private manners can only be transmitted by women, and the so-called "matriarchal" privileges do not fall under the jurisdiction of "patriarchal" courts of law. This fatal dehiscence in the gregarious instinct of civilizations was denounced by St. Paul. Uranism is essentially "antisocial." The Platonism of men and the Sapphism of women lead to the formation of extra-legal conspiratorial and revolutionary groups of coolies, convicts, spies, initiates, and mediums. The apparent exchange of consents between the two parties only unites two complementary intentions of mental misrepresentation. Angelicism, ideal at the outset, quickly leads after insatiable and sterile embraces, to the psychic nexus of a pact which strangles sincerity, to the consciousness of a "possession," to the mental invasion of an overbearing alien intention, envious and perverse, that of a fallen angel, proposing to the possessed soul an escape from the bonds of matter, which is only a lure. According to Scripture, this is a crime that cries out unto heaven for vengeance. History notes certain periods which undergo this kind of crisis: that of Thebes, in Greece, which begins with the abduction of Chrysippus by Laius, continues with the incest of his son Oedipus, and ends with the sacrifice of the Theban legion at Chaeronea; that of the Quattrocento, which begins with Gilles de Rais and Ulrich of Jungingen, and ends with the martyrdom of a remarkable Dominican, Girolamo Savonarola, the savior of Florentine youth.

It is from within this temptation that prayer must call forth the remedy, for its origin is noble, being spiritual, arising out of a pure spirit; though doubtless it is not without bad intention, since it urges humanity to resign itself not to loving transcendence, but to finding consolation instead in an asexual friendship wherein the two partners recognize that they have been formed out of the same clay and thus attempt to recover that primitive unity of the human species which was broken by the wound in Adam's side whence sprang Eve. This dangerous attraction can only degrade if carnal acts, as in the case of the Marquis de Sade, plunge it into a sterile rage of destruction. In its origin, its pure state, however, this friendship of human connaturality is not "unnatural." If it deepens in modesty and chastity, it can arrive at the point of conceiving a vow of virginity and of loving it; for this pure idea infuses itself into human nature like an intellectual light without injuring it, *januis clausis,* when generative sexuality wounds it. In the end, this connatural friendship becomes complementary to transnatural love which unites us with God, and it is an image of the second twilight of Paradise, the permitted upholding of the pact of loyalty.

In order to reach that point, however, we must understand that this pact is not all of the hospitality which God asks us to give to our neighbor, to the stranger, to the uncircumcized, to the "guest" of God, in whose name God Himself will receive us at the Last Judgment ("I was naked and you clothed me . . ."). In offering to substitute himself for the allies of Lot through prayer, Abraham understood this. But the people of Sodom did not accept even the sacrifice of his own daughters which Lot was willing to make for them in order to save his guests from their outrageous behavior.

If there had only been ten righteous men in the accursed city it would have been saved. This prayer of Abraham hovers forever over societies doomed to perdition in order to raise up in their midst those ten righteous men in order to save them despite themselves. And we must believe that at times Abraham's prayer finds ten righteous men so that they, like Capernaum, might be spared the heavenly fire. One could say a great deal about his heavenly fire which is the sign, as expressed by the Semitic languages which have been the instrument of divine revelation, especially the second Semitic language, Aramaic, the language in which the Gospel was preached, the first international language (of artisans and scribes), the language of the special examination in the grave, of which the Muslims speak symbolically.

In his second prayer—at Beersheba, which means "the well of the oath," where God imposed the expatriation or the "he-

gira" upon his first-born son, Ishmael – Abraham consented to
this exile in the desert, provided that Ishmael's descendants
could survive there, endowed by God for their life in this world
with a certain privileged perpetuity which distinguishes that
Ishmaelite Arab race with a vocation to the sword, to "iron,
wherein is mighty power" (Qu'ran 57:25), which, with the birth
of Islam, held sway over all idolators. Against the latter implacable holy war has been declared so long as they do not con-
fess that there is only one God, the God of Abraham – "the first
Muslim." It is a militant vindication of pure transcendence,
a mysterious resurgence of the patriarchal worship which preceded both the Mosaic Decalogue and the Beatitudes, a de-
nudation in the desert which overwhelmed Foucauld. For Islam,
every temporal peace that is not based on recognition of the God
of Abraham is a sham. And even with the Christians and the
Jews, whom they tolerate, the Muslims envisage accord only as
an overhanging ordeal, as a "capitulation" which turns them
into vassals, abandoning contemptuously to these two groups
everything in economic life that plays idolatrously upon the
"facts of God," maritime insurances, indirect taxes, trade in
precious metals, usury, stock markets. . . . The Muslim does
not want these advantages, which are as suspect in his eyes as
are the religious privileges over which these two groups gloat.
He intends to remain God's soldier who demands no pay other
than his lawful part of the spoils of war. The reverse of the holy
war, which is obviously infinitely more noble than wars for
sugar, oil, or potash, is that it leads to the exploitation practiced
by the tolerated Jews and Christians and to the methodical self-
enslavement of idolators. It is from Islam that Christendom borrowed certain aspects of the Crusades and, later, the *asiento* of
black slaves sent to the New World. But, then, all homicide,
which is professional among soldiers, cries out to the heavens
for vengeance.

In the Islam of the descendants of Ishmael there is a way
to achieve salvation – through the *hajj* (pilgrimage). Holy War
is only for men; for women "the *hajj* is the holy war." Now, the
hajj is explicitly based on Abraham, and beyond the animals
whose throats are slit and who are offered up as sacrifices, there

is, from the eve of the immolation of the animals, the pure offering of each pilgrim's heart: at Arafat, where it is offered for the entire community, present and absent (whose names it cries aloud). At that moment, woman is the equal of man. Expanding the Jewish Passover, of which it is not a jealous racial recapitulation, the Islamic *hajj* to Mecca is essentially a spiritual sacrifice at Arafat, and the "descent of mercy" does not wait for the sacrifice of the animals the next day in order to obtain the plenary indulgence (whose "Abrahamic validity" was accepted by the great Jewish scholar Maimonides), thanks to the intercession of pure, humble, and hidden souls. Thus, one day each year, the life of the community is purified, thanks to serene tears, a privilege of the worshippers of transcendence who know nothing of the unhealthy regrets of Western romanticism. The history of the Arab race begins with Hagar's tears, the first tears shed in the Scriptures. Arabic is the language of the tears of those who know that in His essence God is inaccessible and that everything is best this way. If He comes into our midst, it is as a Stranger who interrupts our normal life, like a moment of rest from work, and then passes on. Some people, attempting to fathom the deepest meaning of the sacrifice of Arafat, find therein a way to union with God, but only individually and at night.

Though Islam, which came after Moses and Jesus, with the Prophet Muhammad, who was a messenger of the harsh tidings of the Last Judgment which awaits all creation, constitutes a mysterious response of grace to Abraham's prayer for Ishmael and the Arabs: "I have also heard your prayer" (for Ishmael), Arab Islam is not a desperate claim made by those excluded from the covenant which will be rejected forever. Islam's mysterious infiltration into the Holy Land does not imply this. Islam indeed has a positive mission. It reproaches Israel for believing itself privileged to the point of awaiting a Messiah who is to be born of its race, a descendant of David according to a carnal paternity. Islam affirms that he has already been born of it, though unrecognized, of a predestined virginal maternity, and that he is Jesus, son of Mary, who will return at the end of time as a sign of the Judgment. Islam also reproaches Christians for not recognizing the full significance of the Holy Table, and for not having yet achieved that rule of monastic perfection, *rahbaniya,* which alone creates the second birth of Jesus within them, anticipated by them in this advent of the Spirit of God, the resurrection of the dead of which Jesus is the sign.

This double claim of Islam against the Jews and the Christians who abuse their privileges as if they belonged to them by right and of themselves, this summons which is as incisive as the sword of divine transcendence, whose unconditional recognition, and this alone, can perfect their vocation of holiness, is an eschatological sign which ought to cause us to revive, with infinite respect, the second prayer of Abraham, that of Beersheba.

In his third prayer, Abraham was at Moriah, traditionally identified with the site of the future Temple of Solomon. This was the place of the offering of Isaac. At great cost to himself Abraham carried out to the limit the oath of fidelity which he swore to God when he entered into the covenant of circumcision. Dedicated to divine justice, Abraham abandoned all. He did not pride himself on his vocation. Before the crucial test of the experience of the divine, he abandoned everything he could think about divinity, even the moral qualification for his acts. But his adherence to God exceeded his comprehension, because the genealogical future which he had sacrificed was restored to him. It remained for him to persuade his descendants to complete the interrupted sacrifice. But neither Isaac, who only let himself be bound for sacrifice because he was seized by a sacred terror, nor Sarah, who, left in ignorance about the "genocide" agreed to by Abraham, was not obligated to make excuses for him, and still less would the descendants of Isaac through Jacob and the Twelve Tribes of Israel be persuaded. It would require the totally innocent abandon of a Virgin Mother without human spouse to accept the obligation to offer up her son unto death. It remains true, however, that by his sacrifice

Abraham gave his race a sacerdotal character and dedicated the Israelites to becoming priests. But pharisaic literalism, which fails to "participate," has made them conduct themselves often as bad Levites, as "antisocial" objects of scandal for the Gentiles. Alongside the philo-Judaism of the Iranians and of the Greeks of Alexandria we also see the growth over the centuries of the hereditary anti-Judaism of the Greeks of Pergamum, Rhodes, and Byzantium, in the face of the Jewish sacerdotal scorn not only for the Samaritans and the uncircumcised, but also for the proselytes as well, who were treated as inferiors, and for the feminine sex, though (because of the Messianic promise) women were less scorned among the sons of Sarah than among the sons of Hagar. The fossilization of the privilege (whether priesthood or nobility), the hypocritical legalism and sacrilege of men, tarnished the history of biblical Israel with an unwholesome color on the outside while within there smouldered an unknown purity, a compassionate resurgence of grace before the Law, among Jewish women. Grace penetrated even through the Law under the fossilization of the privilege (priesthood) and under the appearance of such sins as incest (Tamar), prostitution (Rahab, Esther, Ruth), adultery (Bathsheba), and leprosy voluntarily contracted by Miriam, Moses' sister, who three times saved her brother from the waters, bringing to Israel the penitential water of all her Mikvahs. And it sparkled with Mary of Nazareth, who offered herself to the Stranger, becoming an object of suspicion all her life, in order that the true Temple which she conceived might retain the stamp of the first Temple, which was built, as Martin Buber reminded me, by the sons of adultery. Nazareth would drive Mary out and erase her name from its Megillot. Bar Kochba would slay all the Jewish-Christians who refused to avow that Mary was an adulteress. And three times—under Constantine (with the Happisses), under Sultan Baibars (of the Mamluks), and now, Nazareth would resound with a legalistic protest against Mary.

From the fourth century A.D. onward, the New Israel, the church, imitating the administrators of the Old Israel wherein the priests were supported by the state in dealing with questions of sacrilege and simony, entrusted to the secular arm the forced imposition of the sacraments without prior conversion of the heart. This method, having enabled her to "colonize" the pagans of Europe, came face to face with the obstacle of Islam; and before taking the Promised Land back from Islam by force, the First Crusade intended to absorb the Jews, the first possessors of Palestine, in its conquest of the cradle of the Messiah of meekness and peace, by baptizing them by force. That took place in the Rhineland where, by an extraordinary act, the Jewish mothers preferred that their little children be strangled by the rabbis, according to a rite of *Akeda,* the binding of Isaac (studied by Leopold Zunz), a baptism of blood, mixing martyrdom with genocide, that revolted me at first, in 1949 (cf. my article in *Dieu Vivant,* no. 13, 1949, p. 26). Then my friend, Rabbi Maurice Liber explained to me the Abrahamic faith which helped those oppressed Jews rediscover God as Father and Son, in place of their own fathers and sons who were sacrificed (I understood the death of my own father and of my eldest son a little better by this). And the upsetting book by André Schwarz-Bart (*The Last of the Just*) about the *lamed* (*Vav Tzassikim*), and the heroic suicide of the Jews of York on March 16–17, 1190.

The dogmatic cruelty of the Christian inquisitor striking against the sign of blood and witness of the Spirit, thought up a compromise through gold, thanks to that verse of the Scriptures (Deuteronomy 23:20) which permitted lending money at interest to the stranger, a verse which Jesus abrogated (Matthew 10:6–10) in order to establish universal brotherhood, but which the Jewish people had applied in founding the colonial bank of the Muslim caliphs and thereby were "bearing the sin of usury for them." Likewise, from the time of the Council of Vienna (October 1311), the Jewish people organized (with a monopoly) the colonial bank of the Christians to replace the bank they had previously organized for Islam. But they did this without foreseeing that in the course of time the pogroms of the colonized and exploited humble people would be diverted against the Jewish usurer, "the sucker of the blood of the poor" (as Bloy

would say), by his depraved accomplices, the evil Christian cler-
ics. All this induced in the milieus of both Jews and Christians
that practiced that unhealthy usurious symbiosis a deep moral
crisis from their sin: through black masses and voodoolike rites
(symbolic deaths such as the Masonic rites of the assassins of
Hiram, the murder of Aman or that of a Christian child in the
circles of the "unnatural" and skeptical Marranos, the black
masses of evil Christian priests). We have elsewhere studied these
degradations whose frequency and social significance may have
been exaggerated by Huysmans. (Cf. the 1962 re-edition of the
1957 issue of *La Tour Saint-Jacques* on Huysmans. Add St.
Eustratius of the Ukraine [1076] to the four cases treated by
Pope Clement XIV.)

Between 1917 and 1948, the reestablishment of the Jewish
people in "Eretz Israel," promised to a Messiah of meekness in
a universal brotherhood implying the abrogation of the privilege of Deuteronomy 23:20, was consolidated, as the saintly Rabbi
Judah Leib Magnes told me, by gold and blood, causing his
brothers once again to fall under the rabbinic *herem* of the (first
Zionist) Congress of Basle, August 1897. For the Jewish people
to become "a universal brother" all that is needed is to renounce
the privilege of Deuteronomy 23:20, not only toward their brothers in Abraham, the persecuted and expelled Arabs, but also
toward all men everywhere. The Jewish people would have to
become an Essene community once again (something presaged
by the discovery of the manuscripts of Qumran as well as by
the discovery of Essenian traces at Ephesus, where Jesus' exiled
mother found refuge). In any case, Marxist criticism sounds the
death knell of the banking economy based on Deuteronomy
23:20, a privilege improperly granted to the *goyim* and abolished by the Messiah (through an apotropaic series of co-sufferers
from within, supported from without by an apotropaic series of
prophets [the thirty-nine of Maimonides] fulminating against
dishonest leaders).

In the last analysis, Abraham prayed that the social pact upon
which cities are founded be pure, that those who are at war ar-

rive at a fraternal peace with justice, and that the priesthood be holy. These three prayers – at Mamre, Beersheba, and Moriah – really constitute one, with the last the seal of the other two. A daughter of Abraham has come: the accursed city had refused hospitality to the Angel-Strangers, and she has received the Holy Spirit, Love, to which one never asks "why" or "how." The race of Ishmael has chosen to make war in the name of a Transcendence that is inaccessible in its peace. She received the salvation of that Peace. The Jewish people have not always resigned themselves to accept in their heart the extraordinary burden of catastrophes which the fasts and penitences that fill their liturgy commemorate. From the beginning she agreed to become a betrothed woman suspected of infidelity, slandered by her neighbors, called an adulteress in the genealogical records of the city where she was born, and suspected (or ignored) for almost 2,000 years by her race for which she had infinite love, because in order to save her people she laid bare the secret vow of an immaculate heart, something that was even greater than Abraham's willingness to sacrifice Isaac. For thus she offered up for Israel the very root of God's justification vis-à-vis His only perfect creature in a spiritual sacrifice unimagined by the angels.

She is also the true Holy Land, being that virgin "clay," predestined, *sublimiori modo redempta,* wherein all of the elect, with their leader, have been conceived. It is therefore she who, like a crestline (and not a dividing line) wherein her appearance can be sensed, draws the pilgrims who seek justice onto the high places of Palestine – Jews, Christians, and even Muslims – without their suspecting it. Like Abraham, these expatriots who have become nomads find their place of election in the Holy Land, and indeed the Holy Land is the last country on earth from which one could drive "displaced persons" into exile without injustice. But jealousy reigns in the Holy Land, along with the industrial development of potash and oil, two intruders into this "kindergarten" of mankind. Palestine has visibly become the center of the world, caught up between the two conflicting power blocs. And in this war of jockeying for position

and influence, the osmotic line of resistance to evil and of healing compassion, that line which Gandhi tried to safeguard for
the people of India by keeping free the places of prayer, always
leads to the horizon in Palestine, to (Abraham's) Hebron, to
(Ruth's) Bethlehem, and to (Mary's) Nazareth and Jerusalem.
It hangs over the Jordanian trench, from the Dead Sea to the
plain of Armageddon on the west, between Mts. Carmel and
Tabor, and, on the east, to the Lake of the Beatitudes.

It is there that we must go to hear, under an unfurling of
desecrations which announce the Judgment, the call of our common father, summoning all hearts which hunger and thirst for
justice to go on pilgrimage to the Holy City; a call repeated
here, after my return from a thirteenth visit, made not without
a great desire, still unfulfilled, to die there.

An Entire Life with a Brother Who Set Out on the Desert: Charles de Foucauld

My colleague, E. Gautier, eminent geographer, professional Saharian, anticlerical humorist, said of Foucauld's exploring of Morocco, that he was possessed with "a layman's passion to understand." In fact, both before and after his conversion, Foucauld's entire life was bent like a bow toward an absolute, toward the Truth.

Being of the Sorbonne, trained in this house of science since 1901, tested by all its demands and still active (in the School of Advanced Studies and the Iranian Institute), I pay homage on behalf of my peers to the scientific, topographic, demographic, and linguistic work of Foucauld: in topography, to his surveys and extraordinary drawings that capture the landscape; in linguistics, to his mastery of Berber dialects of the Sahara; and to his autodidactic method—a bit awkward but powerful—based on an exhaustive technique (admired much by René and André Basset, two masters of the subject).

There is a deeper level of intelligence, however, in which Foucauld, when he became a believer, was an explorer and an exceptional discoverer. This is the level of religious psychology, of that true missiology that is the experiential discovery of the sacred in others and, in response, of holiness in oneself. Charles le Coeur, a sociologist who was killed while in the Italian army and a Sahara expert himself (see *Le Rite et l'Outil,* a thesis submitted in 1939), made the point that it was in this respect that I, an "academic," had become a disciple of Fou-

Delivered as a talk at the Sorbonne on March 18, 1959.

cauld. It is true. Foucauld brought me out of the classic problem of the relationship between science and faith, starting from pure theory and ending in what I have observed and lived of the clash between the opposing monolithic monotheistic faith of the Muslims and the perforating technology of Western culture's colonial penetration. This "shock" made first one, then the other, and also Ernest Psichari, rediscover the Christian faith in the wound of a divine compassion between fighters who had become brothers.

I feel obligated to explain to you how, through this living experience of the sacred in others, Foucauld was given to me like an older brother and how he helped me to find my brothers in all other human beings, starting with the most abandoned ones. Like all contemplative people, Foucauld had not sought the philosophical and theological training necessary to set forth doctrinally the stages of the inner life (for which Huvelin and Crozier, to whom he introduced me, gave him the correct terminology). The latter was not what attracted me to him. Rather I needed him to communicate to me, through spiritual contact, in very simple words, by interviews and letters, his experiential initiation into the real understanding of the human condition, his experiential knowledge of the compassion which drew him and committed him to the most abandoned of human beings. For my own experience made me feel that the most abandoned of people in the most symbolic metaphysical sense of the most sublime negative way are the Muslims: these mysterious people excluded from the divine preferences in history, though the sons of Abraham, and driven into the desert with Ishmael and Hagar. I felt that their temporary exile was the prefiguration of the penitential life of hermits, of solitaries who would sanctify all Muslim generations, fulfilling for them the sacrifice of the Kurban, obtaining by their brotherly compassion the coming of Mercy.

Foucauld was not constituted to vocally evangelize by propagandistic sermons. A messenger in our perverse times in which every expression is corrupted by technocracy, he came to share the humble life of the most humble, earning his daily bread with them by the "holy work of his hands," before revealing to them, by his silent example, the real spiritual bread of hospitality that these humble people themselves had offered him, the word of Truth, the bread of angels, in the sacrament of the present moment. Beneath the tissue of empirical facts he would have them divine the transcendent act. Already his contemplation saw the temporal torn aside by the invasion of the eternal.

This experiential knowledge of the sacred is not a ready-made science; it is an understanding, an interiorization, which cannot be communicated by external means but by acceptance through the transfer to ourselves of the sufferings of others. It is impossible to undertake a study of this knowledge indirectly by gathering statistics on the frequency of cases of compassion, whose existence psychologists and sociologists do not deny though they dispute any religious interpretation of them. Among believers, the directors of souls know very well that one cannot build the administrative life of a community on these hidden charisms, but to the souls who have experienced them, they recommend honoring them as pure spiritual ideas, as a call to go out of themselves toward others, to love fraternally outside their own milieu and their relationships in time and space, here on earth, in a fraternalization that is directed toward the universal. For these sufferings from compassion are the signs of the predestination of everyone to a higher, immortal life. "Whoever's heart lives by love, cannot die."

I cannot speak to you therefore of the outward, physical contour of Foucauld's and my relationship, especially given our apparent lack of results in organizational and numerical terms, but only of the luminous spiritual traces, the divine ransom of our failures, that my memory preserves: the unforeseeable, irreversible, and irrefutable coincidences (at least for the two of us) that have woven a constellation of tiny weblike threads between our two vocations and our two destinies.

The very day I got engaged, with the approval of Foucauld, who then, however, lost hope of my living in Acekrem, I also devoted myself unconditionally to the humble sodality he was trying to establish in the hope it would survive after his death.

I sensed he was alone and I could not abandon this poor man for the sake of starting my family.

This was October 15, 1913. How did I come to this decision? My passion for Africa dated from childhood. At twelve I was subscribing to the *Bulletin of the Committee of French Africa* (a member of the Committee until 1940). My family had ties to Algeria through my mother's godfather, Dr. Quesnoy, who had been a physician in the military there and had died as general inspector of Les Invalides. Then, after my father had stayed there, my ties were with his friend Georges Favereaux of the cabinet of Tirman, with officers of the African army, including Colonel Henry de Vialar, Colonel Henry de Castries (son-in-law of La Moricière and friend of the O. Sidi Cheikh and of Foucauld), and Commandant Alfred Le Chatelier, who had created Ouargala and established at the Collège de France the chair in Muslim sociology in which I succeeded him for thirty years and from where he had organized our entrance into Morocco through investigations for which he made me his partner. These inquiries were carried out in the hard-boiled technocratic, developmental "native affairs" style, in opposition to the [more interpersonal and humane] school of Lyautey, which eventually triumphed and which I and Castries preferred, in terms of style, charm, and noble feeling for Islam.

I was in Algiers in 1901; Morocco in 1904, when I was twenty, to site check my study of the Guilds of Fez in the sixteenth century. My caravan was attacked; I was betrayed by my Arab interpreter; I vowed to learn Arabic (*I am still learning it!*); I stopped drinking wine. When I checked my itinerary that I had prepared in Paris, I realized how infinitely superior were the surveys of Charles de Foucauld. I noted this; and in 1906, when my book was published by S.H.A. in Algiers, I wanted to thank Foucauld. I asked H. de Castries, "Is he alive?" "Yes, but he is a failure, living as an independent priest near Beni-Abbès." I pressed him further and his tone changed: "Lyautey, who has been appointed to Ain Sefra, is dining here tonight; he will take your book to Foucauld." To my very commandeering introduction Foucauld answered similarly (it was the style of the time) but, noting it was the first time he was offered a gift dealing with his dear Morocco, he added to his praises of my documentation: "I pray to God for you with my poor and unworthy prayers. I beg Him to bless you, your work, and your entire life."

At that time I had lost any traces of faith, but this alms from a poor man was accepted; then forgotten. Two years later it came back to me; two years of Arabic language work and of moral crisis: in Egypt, including archaeological work along with some high escapades on the side disguised as a fellah in the company of outlaws, driven by desire to understand and to conquer Islam at any cost. I left Cairo, which was too European, for Baghdad. There I became head of an official archaeological mission, but my life was that of an ascetic in disguise, under the protection, the *aman,* of an Arab family of distinguished Muslims. I next assumed vaguely the disguise of a licensed Turkish officer and went on horseback into the desert in search of ruins located between Kerbela and Nedjef (those of al-Okheidir). There I was caught (amidst the preparations of the Turkish revolution of 1908), arrested, accused of being a spy, beaten, and threatened with execution. I tried to commit suicide because of the horror I felt about myself when, in sudden meditation, my eyes closed before an inner fire which judged and burned my heart; I felt with certainty a pure, ineffable, creative Presence suspending my sentence through the prayers of invisible persons, visitors to my prison, whose names disturbed my thought. The first name was my mother's (she was at the time praying in Lourdes), the fifth was the name of Charles de Foucauld. I was saved by my hosts at their own risk: *dakhala, ijara, diyafa.* After a great many obstacles, I returned to France.

My second thanks sent to Foucauld: I went back under the protection of his prayer as an older brother. He also had been in disguise and taken for a spy (though his only scientific passion was to fill a void on a map of the Moroccan Middle Atlas region), and he also had been saved by his hosts, two guides, Hadj Bou Rhim and Bel Qasem el Hamouzi. He cried out to them (in 1888): "You to whom I owe my life, will I ever see you again?" I too, disguised, was treated as a spy (an indiscreet observer), saved by my hosts, but not only by the living (one was dead, Hallaj, the mystic and martyr of Islam who died crucified for the pure, inaccessible love of God; I would write my doctoral thesis about him, begun then in Cairo). My first tremulous prayer was made in Arabic and in prison, offered as a vow for the salvation of a Muslim friend, a renegade driven to despair, and through him and Hallaj for all my Muslim friends. "The one who loves becomes dependent on the one who is loved" (Péguy). How could I explain all that to Foucauld, who had barely thought about the Arabic Qur'an and who preferred Berber to Arabic, although his last words were *"baghi maut,"* "I am going (or I wish) to die," in Arabic. But he had a hold on me: he was the one living person *named* to explain to me the desire for the desert and "our special duties" toward the Muslims.

November 29, 1908: I finished (after five months' hesitation) my letter to Foucauld. His response, February 8, 1909: "Dear Brother, your letters make me praise God, make me give thanks. I pray for you to the Eternal Beloved. . . ." He also made known his forthcoming return to Paris (his first after eight years in Africa). Arriving for four days, he came at once to my home. He took me to receive the blessing of Havelin, who was incapacitated. Then he plunged me for a whole long and somber night without relief into that glacial and haughty tomb that is the Church of Sacré-Coeur (February 21–22, 1909). After his departure, he launched his first purple brochure (the Association of Sacré-Coeur). Checkmate. We had promised to pray for each other every angelus (*azan*). Foucauld continued to write me his life-plan relevant to me.

September 8, 1909:
   1) to finish his monograph on the Touaregs' language and folklore;
   2) to live in friendship with them;
   3) to receive me in Acekrem;
   4) a secret final vow to succeed him –?

Second trip of Foucauld to Paris, February 23–25, 1911. Masses at Saint-Augustin. Foucauld had General Laperrine write to G. Maspero, my main boss in Cairo, to have me sent on a mission in the Sahara (without my prior knowledge). 1912: on the advice of two great orientalists of the time, Goldziher and Snouck, King Fuad invited me to the new Muslim University that he was founding in Cairo. My director thought that the call of God for me was there, not in the Hoggar; forty classes in Arabic on the history of philosophy *in toto.*

1913: third and last trip of Foucauld to Paris. Lunch in Clichy at the home of my dear Abbé Daniel Fontaine, who "closed the eyes" of my dear first spiritual master, Huysmans, and carried on the sacerdotal work of Père de Clorivière, the Jesuit chaplain at the guillotine in the time of Terror. (Fontaine gave his support to Foucauld on that day, as I learned later.) Two days later, to commemorate the anniversary of his great uncle who was martyred with the Carmelites during the Terror, Foucauld took me with him to serve his mass in the crypt of the Carmelites; but once there, a strange sign from God passed between us like a sword. . . . And a few days later, when Foucauld wanted to have Cardinal Amette bless his project for a spiritual community, he was quickly shown the door. His kindly secretary and supporter, Abbé Laurain, became discouraged (Countess de Flavigny said, "Charles always goofs!").

January 1914: my marriage and honeymoon to Monserrat and the Sahara. Foucauld was supposed to have met us at Insalah, but the head of the station at Touggourt did not allow our car to go further, because driving conditions were too dangerous.

February 23: the return trip through Maison Carrée, where Monsignor Léon Livinhac, the General Superior of the White Fathers and the only person who would support the "Foucauld Association" after his death, blessed my marriage under the sign of Charles de Foucauld, who had just promised to me his "Directory" that I eventually published in 1928, after waiting twelve years for the *imprimatur.* I did, however, publish some excerpts from it in Cairo in 1917 and the whole of it in Tokyo later (Abbé Totsuka translated it into Japanese in 1929; a second edition was given to me in Tokyo in 1958). It was only in 1950 (at Tamanrasset) and in 1955 (at Beni-Abbès) that I was able to bring my wife to complete our planned journey of 1914 to visit the Sahara hermitages of Foucauld.

1915: departure with the First Zouaves [French battalion of Algerian Light Infantry dressed in oriental uniform], sent with the C.E.D. to the Dardanelles, August 4, became intepreter attached to the Air Force (port of call 98T, ground personnel), then to the H.Q. which became the 17th H.Q. Division of the Colonial Infantry in Macedonia, where I decided to volunteer for service (October 4 and 9, 1916) in the frontline trenches (as second lieutenant T.T., then T.D.; was head of a battalion of reserves in 1939). I wrote to Foucauld of my wish to volunteer, asking him if this decision seemed right to him (in my heart, my letter was a feeble attempt to show him that I had not deserted his call, but would he understand?).

My third spiritual contact with Foucauld: his letter of December 1, 1916, written a few hours before his death (according to Mesdames de Bondy and de Blic and to General Laperrine), expressed his joy that I had chosen "danger, hardship." I experienced the desire he, a retired officer, knew: "May God protect your life, which I ask of him with all my heart. . . ." By a strange switch, he was killed and I was protected. I received this letter, preserved carefully for me by my wife, only later. On January 27, 1917, the anniversary of our marriage, a letter from my wife included a clipping from the *Temps: Foucauld killed in Sahara.* Beside myself, I climbed onto the parapet of the snow-covered trench, seized by a feeling of sacred joy, and cried out: "he found his way, he succeeded!" Some days later, my permission to return to Paris. Monsignor Le Roy, who was recommended to me by Monsignor Livinhac, had saved the "Association." And in response to his request for a biography, I told him I felt that René Bazin should write it. (Foucauld had given Bazin my name in the only letter he wrote to him.)

How many times since 1917 have I received visits from persons unknown to me sent by Foucauld. . . .

How many times have I been taken again beyond the realm of the dead by the angelic contact of the soul of Foucauld, in a state of muffled shock, blinded by a percussive compassion, taken along the road of the Good Samaritan from Jerusalem to Jericho (which I walked on again for the thirtieth time last January 31), answering a call to represent France on Holy Thursday 1918, in the Holy Sepulcher during the siege of Verdun; inquiry as a reporter for the Interministerial Commission for the centenary of Algeria, in 1929; restoration of the Poor Clares of Nazareth in the convent that he had loved, February 6; defense of the purity of his dear Nazareth, here in the Sorbonne on June 17, 1948; renewing of the traditional vow of the Sorbonne professors (prior to 1789) to defend the Immaculate Conception; visits to prisons. All of this without any grand material results.

And so many other humanly disheartening coincidences of grace in which Foucauld met me again to exhort me, as he had written me on October 30, 1909, to make with Jesus to his Father "a declaration of love, of pure love, in the spiritual dryness, the night, the estrangement, the appearance of abandonment, the self-doubt, in all the bitterness of love, without any of its sweetness."

He had hoped to find through me a means to make his Sahara work survive, though I would have been only a footbridge for shortening his path of abandonment and spiritual detachment. Marie Moitessier, Madame Olivier de Bondy, his cousin, his great friend, his favorite sister, assured me that Foucauld had believed to the end that I would come to pray with him in the desert. She asked me to help her bequeath his chalice to a nun whom I had recommended to her (R. M. Marie Charles de Jesus, foundress of the Mazes, who died in exile on November 9, 1961, in Brussels) in "Soledad," which his Indian daughters of Trivandrum entered that same day, and thus to place in good hands the votive offering that Foucauld had entrusted to her. I lit candles for him again at La Madeleine and at Sainte-Baume with D. Jourdain.

One of the last "calls" from Foucauld was in 1950 when I went to Tamanrasset to complete with my wife the journey of our honeymoon interrupted at Touggourt in 1914. We went by military plane that transported food to the fortified outposts of the eastern Sahara, the Grand Erg, Fort Flatters, Fort Polignac, Ghat (where I spoke with Madani ag Soda, the last survivor of Foucauld's murderers), Djanet, Bir el Gharama, and Taman-rasset. At the latter, during the night of October 19–20 from 11 P.M. to 4 A.M., I had my *night of adoration with Foucauld in his Borj;* a dark night, darker than our first night of adoration together in Sacré-Coeur in 1909; in greater poverty and more reducing of myself to ashes. But an Arabic proverb says, "God is able to see a black ant crawling on the black stone at night," *dabib al-nimlat al-sawda, 'ala al-sakhrat al-samma, fi'l-laylat al-zulma.*

In my prayer united with his and in my sacrifice blended with his sacrifice, I hold the whole mass of Muslim faithful for whom he died, for whom for more than fifty years my life has been given fraternally and by whom his life was taken violently. Both of us had entered their home protected by the *aman,* the sacred hospitality; both of us had abused it, we used it, in disguise, in our layman's passion to understand, to conquer, to possess. But our disguises had given them to us unspeakably by that right of asylum that no man of honor, especially no outlaw, can betray, for it is his last virginal point: his honor as a man. Some have compared Foucauld to Lawrence of Arabia, and even have dared say, believing it as praise, that both had abused the Arab and Muslim hospitality. Now, I knew Lawrence well, Thomas Edward Lawrence; we were both appointed adjunct officers of Emir Faisal in Jiddah. He confided to me in our car on the day of the capture of Jerusalem that if he gave up his rank, if he died voluntarily in abjectness, it would be out of disgust at having been a representative of our alliance with the rebelling Arabs, whom we used, then betrayed, as if it had been all right for a man of honor to turn his hosts over to their enemy.

I think sometimes that Foucauld respected the host and his right of asylum, a sacred respect for a priest, so much so that if he decided at the end to keep a weapon in his Borj, he who had vowed never to have any weapon in his cell, it was because he was giving to his enemies "full dispensation to shed his blood" in a lawful sacrifice.

Foucauld changed for them in advance the designation of their murderous act: "be the fighters of a holy war, and I will die a martyr." He was thereby entering into their hearts as an inebriating wine. Jesus, already broken on the cross, was destroyed even further in offering his last fraternal meal, poor fragile relic, frail wonder, revered object, which is neither an ikon nor an idol since he gave himself completely broken and dying to make us live again, we his enemies, his murderers, his hosts in the poor paradise of his heart.

"Put yourself like a brand on my heart, put yourself like a brand on my nailed arm, for love is as strong as death, and the fire of its jealousy is harder than Hell."

My Entry into Jerusalem
with Lawrence in 1917
(1960)

A second lieutenant in the colonial infantry, I was promoted temporarily to the rank of captain, on March 15, 1917, and attached to the Franco-British Sykes-Picot mission, to work on the implementation of accords signed in London in 1916 between Great Britain and France under the auspices of Lord Kitchener: to establish the zones of French and British influence in the Near East. I was chosen as one of the mission's three French adjutants because I was an Arabist and Islamist; the other two, Gaston Maugras and Robert Coulondre, were career diplomats. Sir Mark Sykes, assistant to Lord Balfour for oriental affairs, had with him only a sort of personal secretary, a Palestinian Arab, G. Albina; but from time to time the future Lord Lloyd was sent to him. Sykes and Picot were in direct contact with London and Paris respectively through coded cablegrams without having to go either through the British commander-in-chief in Cairo (General Murray and, later, General Allenby) or the French ambassador in Cairo.

I arrived on April 21, 1917, at Port Saïd (via Rome) and the mission put me in touch immediately with the army and with some Arab individuals. Sir Mark Sykes (who became very friendly towards me and to whom I owe, as I mentioned at the time of his premature death in Paris [*Revue du Monde Musulman,* 1919, pp. 15–22], my initiation into the remarkable British understanding of an international community in which the rights of small nations to exist would be safeguarded, an understanding foreign to most geopoliticians of the European continent) tested me by having me write the minutes of five diplomatic conferences held on board the *Northbrook* (we were the guests of the naval commander-in-chief, Admiral Wemyss). Three of the conferences were held between Wejh and Jiddah with Emir Faisal (May 16–18), two with King Hussein (May 18–20 en route from Jiddah). That was the beginning of my friendship with Emir Faisal, a trusting friendship that lasted until his death and which made me the guarantor of the agreement signed between him and Clemenceau in Paris on January 6, 1920, an agreement that was subsequently broken by Gouraud at Meisseloun in a betrayal which Berthelot sent me to investigate, at considerable risk to myself.

These beginnings convinced Sir Mark to treat Lawrence and me equally and to appoint us both adjutant officers of the Arab commander of the northern army, a unit which was then forming and which would be assigned to Emir Faisal at the time of the seizure of Gaza. This promotion issued simultaneously from the British Foreign Office and from Quai d'Orsay, but such could be operational only if the developing military situation permitted the balance of Anglo-French forces provided for in the Sykes-Picot accord to be maintained. Soon after, the failure of General Murray to take Gaza forced the four British divisions to be transferred from north of the Aegean to Egypt, obliging France to send to the Gaza front only the small detachment of Colonel de Piépape, thus dividing the eastern theater of operations between Sarrail (Macedonia) and Allenby (Egypt and Syria).

Furthermore, Lawrence, who had already done excellent fieldwork, had to agree to my appointment, and he had been forewarned against Sir Mark by his comrades in the Arab Bureau of Cairo (the Intelligence Service that was as stupidly Francophobic as ours was, despite my efforts, Anglophobic and Arabophobic).

Sir Mark, nevertheless, tried with the help of Clayton, a man of class, to get me accepted in the circle of British officers of the Arab Office, who put me to work on the admirable regional

Handbooks compiled by their R.S. since Doughty (condensed in 1929 to 708 pages Volume I of the *Handbook for Arabia*). Thanks to this study I was able to conceive the French *Annuaire du monde musulman*. I spoke of Iraq with Leachman and especially with Hogarth, "manager" of the "colt" Lawrence, who explained to me the latter's "behaviorism," his undisciplined and exciting wildness, and how, in order to make him write his mission reports in the desert, Hogarth had to bolt the door and wrestle with him to make him sit and dictate intelligible answers to his questions.

One day, August 8, we were placed in each other's presence, alone, at the Arab Bureau for about two hours, just Lawrence and me. He was already a legend to me. I discovered, with some surprise, a still very young-looking Englishman, free of every convention, almost an outlaw, but very direct, simultaneously sweet and bitter—with a shyness comparable to a young girl's, followed by harsh intonations uttered in a whisper, almost like a prisoner. We sounded each other out first in French, then in English, and finally in Arabic, for a rather long time, not without slips: after three months I had gotten back my Arabic in the style of *al-Manar,* a modernist Muslim journal, but it was overlaid with that of *salafism,* the old style, and a tinge of mysticism. He was answering me in a clipped, intense, and not too correct broken dialect. I was naively a theorist of an Arab Muslim *kriegspiel,* and Lawrence felt that this would give me a considerable influence over Faisal, to his own detriment. He tried honestly to put himself in my position, and shared with me certain political confidences about the Hashimite family, such as the secret plan of King Hussein to have himself declared, not caliph, but imam, in the manner of the Zaydi Shi'ites of Yemen. But this was the extent of his knowledge of Islamic *usul al-fiqh.* He counterattacked, trying to make me return to the intellectual mask of a wandering archaeologist, but nine years had passed since Okheidir. From this day on, I felt that Lawrence avoided any effort to be close. "You like the Arabs more than I do," he concluded.

At the end of September 1917, after an "interval" during which

I read about the Catalan renegade Anselme de Turmeda (Ibn al-Turjuman) in his *Présent de l'homme lettré,* a fiercely Muslim book, Sykes and Picot sent me out to the Suez Canal, opposite Ismailia, on the east bank, to the camp where Ali Khulqi and Nouri Saïd were forming the Arab legion which would go up again with Faisal from Aqaba, at the right moment, to Tafileh and Maan. I wrote a sociological study of these "volunteers," among whom there were even some Christians from Mosul and some Jews from Yemen, both of whom deserted soon after. I became friendly at the time with Fuad al-Khatib, a member of an important family in Hebron, English educated, whose Gallophobia I "defused."

Suddenly one day I received an order to go to Kalab, near Gaza, to the Great Headquarters. At the edge of that enticing desert of forbidden Arabia to which I had given myself as an outlaw nine years earlier on a very primitive and very naked impulse, I awaited my fate, which was in the hands of Lawrence. I had no illusions: my chiefs wanted to give me a large budget to "corrupt Syrian bedouins"; I was supposed to bring them gold; I was sure I would be assassinated. Even surer was my feeling of being damned for buying friends, I who had known the sacred hospitality of the Arabs. I had just carried to Suez (September 18 with G. Maugras) 950 thousand francs in gold to King Hussein, and Sharif Nasser told me later how Lawrence, in an alarming gesture of contempt, was throwing guineas into certain outstretched hands, for all their "hardships." To have left the front and the 56th R.I.C. for that!

On October 11, I was received by Clayton, and afterwards by General Bols, chief of the Great Headquarters. The next day, the 12th, I had two very long talks there with Lawrence, in a tent in the desert. He talked, not of a future to be built with others, but of a kind of solitary space for two in a strange detachment from the world. He brought to mind a kind of elemental freedom forged out of an asceticism so utterly withdrawn that my own naked faith was shocked by the presence of his *no man's land.*

On October 13, General Bols summoned me and told me,

on Allenby's behalf, that he had decided to cable the Foreign Office his refusal to give Lawrence and me our joint appointments under the Arab commander of the northern army (Lawrence later chose Pisani, who had no feel for diplomacy). If Lawrence had come back by plane from Aqaba the day before, it would have been to say he would resign if he and I were both appointed to Faisal. I was told that Lawrence had already worked too long in the field to be taken seriously (did Lawrence perhaps not want me to get killed?). General Bols commented, not without humor, that one was not always in agreement with Lawrence and that Allenby had told him to introduce me to the one who had just warned him that "Lawrence had bet on the wrong horse."

It is against this background that I went to greet Philby in his tent. The latter had just come out of the S.R. of the Indian army and was bent on persuading Great Britain to play the Saudi card, not the Hashimite card (of course, seven years later, Philby came with Ibn Saud as conqueror of the Hijaz; and twenty-five years later, the U.S.A. took possession of the Saudi map from Great Britain, along with its petroleum).

Philby lacked the class of Lawrence and learned Arabic very slowly; but he had foreseen accurately, contrary to Lawrence, that only the Saudis had a loyal military and social infrastructure in Arabia.

My comeuppance on Lawrence came very soon. In 1919 Lloyd George, to the furor of Lawrence, "abandoned" Faisal to us. On November 18, 1919, the Emir, who had received signs of my loyalty during 1918–1919 in Damascus, asked that I be put in charge of the negotiations for the Franco-Syrian treaty; but neither my letter of service signed on December 1, 1919, by Berthelot in the name of Clemenceau, nor the signed agreement of January 6, 1920, prevented the treachery of colonialism from making us break our promise at Meisseloun.

My last meetings with Lawrence were in December of 1917 (at the time of his death, I wrote to Deedes, who answered me with a very interesting letter: "he had to die like this"). On December 9, 1917, I saw him in the camp at Gaza; he was already

anxious about the future of the Arabs. He felt – and accepted
the idea – that we would be given Lebanon, but nothing more.
On the 10th, the High Commissioner F. G. Picot was summoned
(he took me; I had sensed this coming three months before) to
the Great Headquarters at Gharbiya (via Deir Souleid) to receive the announcement of the surrender of Jerusalem. On December 11 came the solemn entry into Jerusalem, for which
General Bols, in order to enable the Sykes-Picot mission and
the Foreign Office to save face, thought of the following order
of protocol: in the first car, Allenby and Picot; in the second
car, Bols and Piépape; in the third car, Sir Wyndham Deedes,
the Supreme Chief of the eastern S.R., a man of rare distinction for whom I have always retained a strong feeling of respect,
Lawrence and myself. Other cars followed in which there were,
along with the British officers, a (phantom) head of the Italian
mission and an American attaché. We stepped out of the cars
at the Jaffa Gate at 10:30 A.M.

I spent the whole morning with Lawrence. The declaration
of martial law in front of the Tower of David – by Allenby –
snatched from the Sykes-Picot mission any power to make diplomatic decisions related to the Holy City (coveted by London
for itself alone). Allenby threatened Picot harshly with arrest
if he interfered with this order. Lawrence stayed close to me;
his defeat was equal to mine, or even worse, and his innate nobility made him open his heart to me. Charged with assuring
King Hussein that the Holy City would be entrusted to him,
Lawrence had just learned about the negotiations of Lord Balfour with Lord Rothschild for a Jewish homeland. His country
had entrusted him with the task of betraying his host, and Lawrence felt it was a sacrilege committed in violation of a promise
given to an Arab, just as I had felt earlier at Meisseloun. Our
entry into the Holy City occurred under the sign of this desecra-
tion. Lawrence was so shocked that, when we arrived together
late at the luncheon held for Allenby in the Great Headquarters, near Ain Karem (in a Protestant school established for the
Christianization [sic] of Israel: Allenby was rather anti-Zionist),
and when we were passing through the large courtyard under

the eyes of the officers, I signaled Lawrence to attach his left shoulder strap. He said, "Do you think that I have any respect for these people?" And at that moment he made a gesture of opening his pants to urinate in front of the headquarters. It was, in a small way, the gesture of Sir Thomas More at the Tower of London, but without its cheerfulness.

The diplomatic mission went back the same day to Gharbiya, returning to settle in Jerusalem on the 14th, and Lawrence went back to Faisal.

Visitation of the Stranger:
Response to an Inquiry about God
(1955)

I am reversing the order of your questions since you allowed me to do so.

1. *The meaning of the word "God," its consequences*

Discovery antecedes theory, commotion precedes denomination.

An internal break in our habits, a brief disturbance of the heart, a point of departure for a new order in our personal behavior; or, if one looks from without, the acknowledgment of a sin, the transgression of the Law. Before the Lord who has struck the blow, the soul becomes a woman, she is silent, she consents and the jealousy of her primordial virginity dissuades her from looking for the "why" or the "how." She starts only to commemorate in secret the Annunciation, viaticum of hope, that she has conceived in order to give birth to the immortal. This frail Guest that she carries in her womb determines thereafter all of her conduct. It is not a made-up idea that she develops as she pleases according to her nature, but a mysterious Stranger whom she adores and who guides her: she devotes herself to Him.

Morally: the soul sanctifies herself to protect her sacred Guest from any defilement by earthly actions, since the Inaccessible

39

has exposed Himself to them by His visit. *Socially:* the soul cannot hide the pure Witness with whom she is "pregnant"; she feels herself marked, "branded," stigmatized by suspicions, the blows which injure Truth and call forth Justice among the oppressed, the imprisoned, slaves and convicts. *Esthetically:* how not to soothe her sorrowful compassion with a song of hope, made with allusions to carefree futures, rich with intelligibility and consolation, and especially to this divine Guest whom she cannot bring to the world before the apocalyptic fullness of time. *Pedagogically:* she does not speak about her Guest "didactically" like the orator who is more or less an actor playing the God of modern biblical exegesis, but rather testimonially, waiting for the moment when He suggests to her that she invoke Him, making her progress in experiential knowledge through compassion.

2. *Our representation of God*

The moment comes for the believer when it is necessary no longer "to conceive" God as a woman conceives, blindly, but to explain the notion one has of Him. With words and names. Very quickly, alas, these become idols to be put on pious display in the profiteering "stock exchange" of "values." Fortunately, One comes sometimes to overturn the vendors' stand – and to show them that the divine *Questions,* even on the purely philosophical plane, exist apart from the exhibited individual solutions. The true *Answers* of humanity are the uprooted words of prayer which are rich with dogmatic definitions (*not yet mummified by theological directives*). "Lex orandi, lex credendi." It is in the bosom of Abraham, beyond the Law, in the sacrifice of the "King of Justice," when Abraham was blessed, that all liturgies inspired by human supplication will rediscover the unique "God," the principle of their unity.

3. *The correspondence of the word "God" in me*

These correspondences do not really exist as "data" in any table of analogical divine attributes. The copula "to be" means *to do as if* God were all in all. What this involves is a mental shift of our center, one that is, so to speak, Copernican, to function in us, or, rather, to be felt. In terms of spiritual cartography, in order to carry out the divine course indicated by fixed landmarks on the rectangular projection of Mercator's chart, one has to get to the axial peak of a conical projection of the world, to the summit of the umbra where all durations will be eclipsed.

The Stranger who visited me, one evening in May before the Taq, cauterizing my despair that He lanced, came like the phosphorescence of a fish rising from the bottom of the deepest sea; my inner mirror revealed Him to me, behind the mask of my own features—those of an explorer exhausted after a ride in the desert, betrayed to his hosts by his scientific gear, the disguise of a spy—before my mirror darkened in the presence of His fire. No name remained in my memory (not even my own) that could have been shouted at Him to free me from His scheme and let me escape His trap. Nothing left, that is, but the recognition of His sacred aloneness: acknowledgment of my own unworthiness, the transparent shroud between us, the intangibly feminine veil of silence which disarms Him and becomes irridescent with His coming: through His creative word.

The Stranger who took me as I was, on the day of His wrath, inert in His hand like the gecko of the sands, little by little overturned all my acquired reflexes, my precautions, and my deference to public opinion. By a reversal of values, He transformed my relative ease as a propertied man into the misery of a pauper. By a "finalist" reversal of effects on causes, of intersigns on archetypes, as most men experience only when dying. And this would be an excuse if I did not propose further, here, to search through the biographies of mystics for an ersatz technical vocabulary in order "to enter into the presence" of the One whom no Name *a priori* dare evoke, neither "You" nor "I" nor "He" nor "We," and if I did not transcribe simply a cry that is of course imperfect but poignant uttered by Rumi (quatrain 143) in which the essential, insatiable, and transfiguring divine Desire flows forth from the depth of our silent and naked adoration, at night:

The One whose beauty made the Angels jealous has come in the morning twilight, and He looked into my heart;

He was crying and I cried until the coming of dawn, then He asked me: "of the two of us, who is the lover?"

Islam and the Testimony of the Faithful

[This study, published in *Esprit*, Paris, September 1953, was preceded by the following:]

The France-Maghreb Committee, recently formed under the direction of François Mauriac, held a press conference in Paris last June 29. Professors Blachère, Massignon, and C. A. Julien, along with General Catroux, spoke on that occasion. A few days earlier the petition of a number of pashas and kaids calling for France to depose the Sultan of Morocco was made public. After the report of Professor Blachère, who explained this manifestation from the angle of administrative legality, Louis Massignon, Professor of the Collège de France, treated it from the angle of spiritual testimony. We requested from him the following transcript of his talk:

The sociological documentation I am reporting on today was gathered directly in the field. I first was in Fès in 1904; my last visit there was in 1946 at the time the commission for educational reform was set up. In the interim, I focused my investigations on the crafts corporations [guilds], especially during 1923–1924, under Lyautey. The problem of the corporations, however, is connected directly to the mystical problem of the brotherhoods, of which I shall speak here, for it is the latter who provide "the lawful bread" to the workers in Islam.

I studied all of this directly in Arabic; first, because I was trained professionally as an Arabist; secondly, and most of all, because I was given the opportunity to live "as an Arab" among Muslims. The "testimonial" vigor of the Arabic language has ever since held my attention.

So, I won't talk about the administrative attributions called into question by the "petition of the Moroccan kaids," but about its testimonial impact from a social point of view — that is, about the canonical testimonies expressed on this occasion by certain Muslim personalities and about their lawful "domain of application." I am concerned with the persons in question only insofar as they are attempting to identify themselves with the powers of their position, that is, out of self-interest.

In support of the aforesaid petition of the kaids, two leading Moroccan personalities came forward: "the President of the brotherhoods of North Africa" (El Kittani) and the Pasha of Marrakesh (El Glaoui). During the month of Ramadan, a month of fasting and recollection, they demanded the deposition of the Sultan, testifying that he was "canonically" unworthy. It is the prior question of the validity of these two testimonies that we shall examine.

"Brotherhoods" — they are mystical congregations. Mysticism, especially in Islam, has a secret and profound impact on social life as a source of purification of wills. The major portion of my researches and publications, in both French and Arabic, examines this impact. So much so that I was once accused [by the Algerian reformist Brahimi in 1950] of having done it all in the pay of our North African S.R. as "head of the fifth column." One gains access to mysticism, however, especially among Semites, only through perfect hospitality, the right of asylum, the *ikram al-dayf*, the philoxeny; whereas the S.R. must deceive the host in order to betray him, thereby excluding himself forever from understanding him in his inner soul, his sworn faith, his testimony of God. God, the God of Abraham and the One of Islam, being transcendent, the Muslim state, founded on a revealed Law, does not trust mystics who deduce from a state of "intimacy" with God in order to articulate, through the theopathic locution as witnesses of God, unusual graces that release the faithful from legal prescriptions. The Muslim state, which doesn't recognize any brotherhood, urges the congregationists not to get mixed up in public affairs, since they have "renounced the world." This is, it must be added, the standard position held by all states vis-à-vis the brotherhoods.

Nevertheless, when the observance of rituals becomes fossilized and the casuists degrade them, the Muslim conscience feels that a mystic's protest must be raised in the name of God to "command what He has ordained and to condemn what He has forbidden." The Christian world also knows this when the regular clergy admonishes a secular clergy that has become decadent. In Islam, it is an isolated individual, a mystic, a "redresser of wrongs," who rebels, a *mahdi* (one who shows the straight path).

It was, I agree, true to Islam for the President of the brotherhoods of North Africa to raise an indignant testimonial cry of protest if he felt that the modernism of the Sultan was a breach of the faith. But why legitimize the outburst of his inner conviction by dressing it up with the conceited and absurd title of "president" of an imaginary federation of brotherhoods that Muslim law ignores and that some very blundering advisors suggested to him? The brotherhood conference at Fès, in fact, assembled delegates from three North African countries to "excommunicate" one of the three "independence" parties, the Moroccan one, which may provide a fatal precedent for us.

This President of the brotherhoods of North Africa at least understood that he had to form his personal oral testimony as a witness of God against the Sultan on his own. Here, I would like us to reflect on the social mechanism of testimony in Islam. Islam is above all an oral testimony, a profession of faith, a *shahada* "in the Name of God." To attest to (or contest), legitimate and "pure" property rights and obligations, Islam has instrumental witnesses, *shuhud 'adl,* attached to all of its courts. Though they have declined to the point of forming a bourgeois class of archivistic notaries, it is still true that what counts in court is not the text of a "chirographer" but their *given word*. And any Muslim who is sound of mind and has reached the age of puberty can and must give testimony, indeed must stand up and honor the legal prescriptions at stake.

Today in Morocco one still finds this prerogative that is both religious and democratic: the testimony of the faithful, and we had three examples of this during the last Ramadan. Let's not forget the danger in disrupting Ramadan (The Netherlands knows it well, since it lost Java because it kidnapped the Muslim president of the new Indonesian state in the middle of Ramadan). The first voice that was raised had a duty to speak. He was the preacher of the cathedral mosque of Fès, Ben Larbi Alaoui, the former Minister of Justice, a man both learned and respected. Our police, nevertheless, arrested him and exiled him on grounds that "reliable witnesses" had heard him "speak against France." The first step of "France-Maghreb" was to ask for the freedom of the preacher who had said the following: "God is served first; do not be 'associators' by connecting profane interests with your service to Him." Which profane interests? Those of the two other "witnesses" of whom we have spoken, the "President of the Brotherhoods of North Africa and the Pasha of Marrakesh."

These two representatives, one of mysticism, the other of the "high administration," believed they could testify validly in mid-Ramadan to the unworthiness of the head of the Muslim community. First, by backing a petition of kaids who draw all of their powers from this very head who appoints them; secondly, by yielding to the suggestions of French administrators who were ignorant enough to think that Moroccan opinion was imbued with the same disingenuous skepticism of Parisian opinion, which would accept the testimony of anybody on anything unless the press dared mention the reasons for possible objection.

The constant rule of the Muslim community of the faithful is to proceed with the prerequisite *purification (tazkiya)* from the mouth of the witness who is going to speak. The mouth is used to speak but also to eat. This is the aspect, which is both mystical and material, of the purification of the intention in Islam: the *ikhlas.* Christians attempt to institute this by means of the confession of "sins" through "examining of hearts," true. But Islam institutes it more simply by examining the pure or impure nature of the witness's mode of living. All of the law manuals have a list of impure professions.

I ask you earnestly to forget the ease of our customs and the progress Europe has made in its tolerance of sinners. We who would propose to delete ruffians from our electoral lists give members of the most pernicious and unspeakable professions the privilege of the military draft and service at the front right along with honest people (which is a scandal, not without reason, to the prelogical mind of primitive peoples). I ask you to forget more: the complacent machinery of forgiveness used by the Christian churches, which tirelessly accommodate hardened sinners — as in cases where chaplains are enabled by secularization to stop excluding persons of infamous professions from ecclesiastical burials. Without noticing it, in giving amnesty to habitual criminals we become the receivers and debtors of their stolen goods.

Islam is both more naively primitive and more fiercely uncompromising than we are. It upholds and sanctions interdictions; it ignores the Durkheimian legerdemain of personal responsibilities. It does not examine hearts; it is satisfied to brandish its list of signs of ritual and social impurity, its list of impure professions that deprive their members of the right to testify. The list is long and seems incongruous, including tavern keepers (wine is forbidden), night watchmen (their police dogs are impure), portuary listmakers, pigeon breeders on roofs (a clandestine postal service for women), and procurers and owners of brothels.

France (even Christian France, alas) has a weakness for procurers. She refused to be part of the international convention of 1949, which defined them as outlaws, in agreement with Islam. Perhaps she hopes, along with Léon Bloy in *Sueur de Sang*, that national heroism can redeem them, as in the case of Denard in Jibouti, and perhaps even, who knows, canonize them. But Islam, which is more naive than we, must stick to formal testimony, to the recitation of the Qur'an, that quite biblical book of interdictions and anathemas which European missionaries have not been able to silence. It is said in the sura of Light, 24:32, *"la tukrihu fatayatikum 'ala'l-bigha'i"* ("you shall not force your slave girls into prostitution").

[Only *Le Monde* had the courage to print this text of mine, on June 30. In Morocco, in its Arabic translation, it met with a great laugh—of relief: for the first time someone dared recall the Qur'an's condemnation to an important "protégé" of that French culture that had forced the Muslims, against their faith, to respect such procurement. In Algeria, at Blida, some Arab women, reading of this citation, cried out in tears that at last there was a voice in France that recognized in the Qur'an the word of truth.]

As in the case of the interdiction of homicide decreed in the Decalogue, one could argue (against me) that commentators have done an excellent job of twisting the meaning of this verse. Unfortunately, the Qur'an is not a silent code of laws for the archives but an oral testimony which cries out when it's consumed.

And in Morocco it cries out, alas, against its nonenforcement due to our failure to uphold the metropolitan law of 1946 against brothels, a failure motivated hypocritically by us on grounds that the Muslims had failed to abolish slavery in Morocco. It is true: Islam accepts slavery, but familial slavery, and at the same time condemns regulated prostitution. I still remember the scandal to the Muslims of Beirut caused by General Gouraud in decorating a well-known slave trader for boosting the morale of the army of the Levant. I remember a young woman whose wedding I had attended and who was kidnapped, on her return from Aleppo, in Marseilles and delivered to a "house" by an elected police official who was never sent to jail. I remember another woman, a Muslim Berber from Beni-Mellal, who, when I passed through there in 1923, I heard cry out to the qadi for help in vain, while her husband was selling her in the used pots market, contrary to the Qur'an but in accordance, the Tarrit commander assured me, with "our" Berber Dahir, who had placed her tribe outside the Qur'anic law.

I am not here to justify Islam for its unjust behavior toward women on other planes, but to state the fact that European colonization is responsible for the systematic establishment of houses of prostitution on Islamic lands. Allenby, for example, in 1917 in Jerusalem, when he was becoming anxious about the rise of homosexuality among his troops, inflicted on the Holy

City the unprecedented shame of that institution prohibited by the Bible: *"ve lo yehye qedesch. . . ."* In fact, the institution seems historically linked to the raising of standing armies (when there are no accompanying women). The barrack paternalism of military leaders regards procurement as an essential "supplementary force" of the supply corps, as I observed in the colonial service, in which I ended up as a battalion head. They assure laymen, however, that it is necessary in order to avoid something far worse, homosexuality, that unadmitted cancer of the North African army, noted by Foucauld in Mascara and by Psichari in Atar.

[An early Muslim belles-lettrist named Jahiz noted its spread among the soldiers of the first Muslim standing army under Abu Muslim. The case of the Teutonic Knights is well known and should lead to a reexamination of the Templars. In Morocco, before the Muslim invasion, it existed among the Berber tribes, and the chaplains of the North African army haven't dared to tackle this dreadful problem openly, one that is even more alarming than regulated prostitution for the welfare of France in the world.] In any case, it is in Morocco that the establishment of large *busbirs* in garrison cities received the greatest degree of complicity by the urban planners (e.g., Agadir). And not without considerable political scheming, if it is indeed true that the Sultan's fatal break with the Residency originated in the bitter fight surrounding the plot hatched in 1947 at the *busbir* of Casablanca to kill Eirik Labonne.

This question of the use of the military *busbir* brings me to the Pasha of Marrakesh. That this high official, who was both decorative and decorated, had been patiently schooled to stand forth as the witness of morality in order to "testify" to the unworthiness of the Sultan, and that he was involved for that purpose in a financial imbroglio that reminds us oddly of the Indochinese scandal of the piaster, is the typical style of the "Arabic Office." But the fact that one ignored Muslim law to the point of disqualifying in advance such a valuable "witness" by encouraging him to increase the taxes that he receives from the prostitutes of Marrakesh (outside the "restricted quarter," a French sector unfortunately), taxes that are contrary to the Qur'an, is an unexpected oversight which reveals the degree of administrative cynicism to which the Muslims of Morocco have been reduced by a capital which persists in neglecting its basic overseas duty: to check abuses, *nazar al-mazalim,* as is said in Muslim law.

It is well known that traffic in women is the most lucrative and most reliable form of slave trade. The nonenforcement of the law of 1946 in Morocco gives a clear conscience to our traffickers over there. The only problem is that of soothing the Muslim conscience of the Pasha, and that is achieved by employing the marvelous evasion of legal responsibilities that constitutes French law as regards limited (liability) companies, which procurers have always used to their benefit in France (especially since the naively cynical issue of the Peyrouton leaflet of December 24, 1940). Since 1933 the Societé d'Urbanisme, founded for a Yoshiwara of 6,000 residents in Guelliz, was guaranteed a support of 50 million [Francs?] from the Pasha, and when it failed in 1936, the influential patrons of the Pasha forced Parliament to reimburse him through the Deposits and Consignments Fund. Other more lasting participants followed, thanks to the concentration of French capital drawn from the female slave trade in Morocco, and these confirmed the Pasha in his role as Muslim and Moroccan "cover" for a limited consortium, a consortium powerful enough to give him credit in Paris in circles of high finance and in Parliament. This disqualified "witness" became the valuable and indispensable "friend" of France whom some attempted to send to the Coronation in London, to the French Academy, and to the poor Livre d'Or of the Municipal Council of Paris.

All this is why, meanwhile, there has been found a second witness to be used to validate the testimony of the Pasha of Marrakesh for public consumption: a theologian, naturally, and a mystic, "the President of the brotherhoods of North Africa," who has deliberately exploited canonical testimony.

This "President," the Sharif Abdel Hayy El Kittani, is not an insignificant figure. As a member of an old noble family and as a man of vast knowledge of tradition and canonical law, he seemed destined to preside over the ulemas of the Qarawiyin in Fès, and, therefore, to be the arbiter of the Sultan's appointments. He was, however, heir of the mystical *"baraka"* of a local brotherhood, the Kittaniya, and he deemed it more profitable to work on establishing a thriving consortium of brotherhoods of North Africa. It is thus as *their* "President" and not as head of the ulemas (who rejected him because of his secret compromises that had gone on for a long time) that he dared to testify, in the Name of God, in favor of the Pasha of Marrakesh.

Has he used this title in this instance because, as one of the ulemas, he knows the canonical unlawfulness of the Pasha's "means of livelihood"? But as a mystic he thinks that a spiritual director can "help" the Pasha and make licit his source of income, especially if he convinces him to give very generous alms to the brotherhood? This forgiving casuistry can sometimes withdraw sinners from their sins, gradually. But the Muslim conscience is much more severe than the average Christian conscience in this regard; it finds it repugnant to make licit the "bread of corruption"; it refrains from drinking at a well that was dug by means of iniquitous labor.

I must in truth declare that in this respect the "President of the brotherhoods of North Africa" exercises his mystical authority with a cynical calm that repudiates such delicacies of conscience. I have had two decisive eyeball to eyeball confrontations with him. The God who guides his conduct is not the God of Abraham, of compassion, of self-sacrifice, of the *"abdal"* (the "substitute saints"). He is, he thinks, the God of personal vengeance (whom Islam has clearly abolished). To bring vengeance upon the Sultan's dynasty (for having atrociously killed one of his parents over forty years ago) he put himself in the service of the French administration in any way he could from the beginning. He became involved with it in ways that were exceedingly reprehensible. He became willingly possessed by his own desires and pride: a simonist, a ventriloquist of God. Should the day come when he will revert to a moral stance, what will he not do to avenge himself against the French administrators who degraded him to such a state in which he acted against everything that Muslim mysticism considers most genuine and most holy? Against the *shahada* itself?

Let's reflect for a moment on the danger that such behavior poses to the French presence and to France's moral authority in North Africa in the future. To use human language as testimony, speaking in the Name of God, merely for tactical propaganda purposes in an uncertainly profitable game of bluff is evidently tempting to the military and to speculators who expect immediate returns. But war and its ruses must give way to peace; and for peace, one must have a diplomacy which seeks to enter with the adversary, as one's questioner, another form of dialogue than bluff. One must try to understand what is best about the questioner – his testimony as a believer – even if and especially if we no longer believe. We must therefore not corrupt him in order to misuse this testimony in our service. Instead of imposing on him, in the name of our cultural superiority, our lowest methods of enrichment and forcing him to assume thereby in the eyes of foreigners our most criticizable attitudes, perhaps we might regain, by contact with this "backward" Muslim Morocco a sense of the sacred, starting with that right of asylum, that generous hospitality, which enabled us to come and settle in his country and which might still permit us to stay, unless we make ourselves wholly disgusting to him.

At the end of this presentation, a member of the audience raised the following question: "How can Muslims accept a declaration made by an "infidel," a kafir, as disqualifying the testimony of a Muslim on the question of procurement?"

Part of Professor Massignon's response is included here: "By asking such a question, a French Christian acknowledges his colonialist's monopoly on the truth, also his moral inferiority vis-à-vis the colonized Muslim whom he regards with the same bias as a customs official. Not aware that there is among men a common Principle of reference, the same God of Truth, the colonialist cannot imagine that a Muslim may feel validly reminded of the observance of a canonical precept that is obviated by a Christian mouth. Such a

Christian does not think that spoken testimony can bring a mutual understanding; he is walled in by his "Pirandellism." But the Muslim, who believes in the original equality of the three Abrahamic religions (Judaism, Christianity, and Islam), knows that they each refer to the same God of Truth. Age-old distortions by them of their own doctrines may have led Jews and Christians to become "infidels," as Muslim apologists argue; but the latter allow that there are also Jewish and Christian souls that are pure, tahirat; that is to say, souls whose testimony is valid because they are transparent to divine light when they read particular verses of the Qur'an, such as Sura 24:32 on the impurity of procurement. Islam consists of testimony invoking the Word of God with purity (ikhlas). If for a Christian this Word is Jesus, for Islam it is the uncreated Qur'an. The testimony of a Qur'anic verse recited as authentic conveys its meaning regardless of the one reciting. The truth shines, it is holy, even if it comes from an infernal mouth, contrary to what a missionary expelled from China told the Secours Catholique: "I denied the use of the word peace to my Marxist questioners because this word in the mouth of a materialist can only mean a lie." How can we ever arrive at understanding if we begin by rejecting any common term? Even one of the most universal, one of our "passions of being" such as truth. According to Islam, in which God is especially the efficient cause, truth, which establishes a relationship, seals every pure testimony.

At the Limit
(Christmas 1956)

At the limit where our beseeching efforts to intercede between two terrorisms finds us overwhelmed and forces us, like Gandhi at Noakhali in 1947, to get down on our knees, let us lift our eyes high toward eternal life, toward the "cloud of witnesses who preceded us." They too were marked and abandoned as hostages and ransoms of justice before its time. They await us as they partake of the chalice of the Passion alone with the Lord, alone with the Essential Desire:

> *Sharibna 'ala dhikr'l-Habibi mudamatan. . . ."* (We have drunk in memory of the Beloved inebriating wine. . . ."–Ibn al-Farid)

Like them, like him, we have had to undergo a "search" and torture, the penitentiary stripping of slaves, to be betrayed by hope, abandoned by the Father, leaving in the heart only the mark of our creation, the *fitra,* an unfissionable atom of faith, *dharra min al-imani,* to reduce our condemned remains to ashes. Such is the faith of the rejected son, the faith of the castaway orphan who can no longer cry, bowed down under his disinheritance by the Mysterious Host who cradled him once in the womb of his mother, in the dreams of his roving nights, and who buries him now in the belly of the earth from which He drew him.

Though buried alive, we still have in our heart the last spark of faith, revived in us more by the gaze of imprisoned criminals than by the look of the self-satisfied and righteous – much more, by the stares of the hunted Muslims than by the glances of the "Christians" and "Jews" who have tracked them down to use

54

as scapegoats. And this when strange theologians in the service
of the secular world doubt that this Muslim faith is theological;
this heroic faith of our father Abraham summoned to sacrifice
his son; this faith of the poor, of the backward, of the ignorant,
hated by our skeptical Christianity; the faith which holds that
there is only one mystery in God, that of His Oneness: the pure
act in which He unifies Himself: *"tawhiduhu 'iyyahu tawhiduhu."*

We want to enter into this pure act through the nonviolence
of the Marian "fiat"; through our Muslim friends, our brothers;
in order to be "one" with them, we their substitutes, as God
is One.

For this abandoned people, there is only one work of mercy:
hospitality; and it is by this alone, not through legal observances,
that we cross the threshold of the sacred. Abraham showed it
to us.

Let's seek it therefore with Abraham among the Muslims,
whom we are driving into the most atrocious despair, in the accursed City where we push them, the City of Essential Rejec-
tion, the City of the Denial of that Hospitality which was asked
of Lot. That is the last spark of faith.

Locked in his outrage as a criminal, pointed at, slandered,
and beaten, in the hyperextension of his whole being, which
shivers under the repugnant precautions of the executioner, we
want to embrace him, though our imperfect substitution may
recoil in horror. It is the truth of *our* wretchedness that speaks
to us on his lips; it is the justice of *our* sentence that binds us
to him with our Savior Jesus.

"Speak the truth even if it burns you with the fire of damnation" (Hariri).

It will not be from our good ruling class, which is skeptical
and lukewarm, which gives excuses and accepts as normal the
worst aberrations on grounds of their being "natural," which
legitimizes the simultaneous extermination of the guilty and the
innocent on grounds of its being "scientific" and "atomic," that
the transfiguring light of the universe will burst forth.

Abraham, the friend of God, had already proposed to Him
ten sparks of faith that are still burning, ten faithful guests re-

siding in the Jordanian Sodom to save it from fire. It is no doubt that from the depth of the spiritual Sodom, from the Hell of "Il Primo Amore" into which Jesus descended in order to re-kindle the extinguished fire of Hospitality, the saving indigna-tion of the Judge will spring.

The Notion of "Real Elite" in Sociology and in History

(1959)

The useful and practical significance of the notion of "real elite" depends on the degree of reality ascribed to the individual person in relation to the group to which he belongs. Is the individual only one of a species, without his own originality? Such is the dictum of certain sociologists, for whom the real elite of a social group is but a chance product of statistical averages "standardized by repetition" (according to the conclusive judgment of Boltzmann). But such a statement robs this real elite of all its real qualities, for it identifies each of the members of this elite with the external relations in the hierarchical scale that differentiate it. Thus the personality of each one disappears and along with it the very usefulness of the notion with which we are concerned in this essay.

It seems to me, then, that sociology ought to go beyond this, and consider the notion of the real elite as an experimental resultant, obtained through investigations into group psychology. There is an inequality among men; a minority exists in every epoch and in every group. The cohesion of this minority has been sustained in a lasting and almost magnetic fashion by its "historical basis of reaction," its social vitality and action of persuasion. We read in Ecclesiastes of a certain person who sud-

From *The History of Religions, Essays in Methodology,* ed. Mircea Eliade and Joseph M. Kitagawa. Copyright © 1959 by the University of Chicago Press. Reprinted with permission.

denly showed himself capable of saving everything when the city was threatened, but fell back again into obscurity when the danger subsided. Posterity is grateful to them, to these superior men, these animators, pace-setters, inventors, and discoverers. They are the "great men" inscribed on Auguste Comte's universal calendar of positivism and, more recently, celebrated on the international calendar of UNESCO. But the cult of such men dies with the earthly cities which they have made flourish through some accidental invention (vanishing like the epidemic that it has wiped out) without much regard for their true personality. In truth, they have accelerated the process of disintegration by over differentiation (and "fission") of the cities and civilizations of the world. They have been able to "insensibilize" their bodies against the sufferings inflicted by disease but, in so doing, have hastened the decay of their spiritual support. It is true that some religions allude to "great souls." Hindus call them mahatmas, Arabians *abdal,* and Christians saints, but they are usually ignored during their lifetime. And so, if their posthumous renown gives to their name a special glory, it is not because of their posthumous life, which spiritists and theosophists have not been able to establish with certainty, but to their apotropaion character. That is to say, they are not isolated in time but become part of a homogeneous series, bearing witness to the same certitude about the efficacy of spiritual means in improving corrupted social and political situations with their sense of compassion for the universal.

How does one establish this? How can one prove that every true human elite is apotropaion? In general, the historians pay very little attention to this. Our ordinary historical documentation comes almost entirely from a class of scribes, generally those concerned with fiscal matters, for whom the official praises of hired annalists are as suspect as the underhanded slanders of apocryphal memorialists. Play-by-play minutes of national parliaments, operational reports from headquarters of intelligence agencies, are worth no more than the caricatures and Pasquinades of "his majesty's opposition." And, as soon as the Marxist party seizes power, it manufactures an official history for political purposes which are even worse. Also a number of our philosophers of history, in their discouragement, reduce the unfolding of events to the mathematical application of an arbitrary axiomatic system of their own invention. Thus they explain the social upward mobility of the inner circle of Caesar or Napoleon in terms incomprehensible to the public of their times. This, in turn, is soon rejected by the founders of a new axiomatic system attempting to explain the evolution of humanity instead of seeking Jungian archetypes, the resurgence of which has coincided with the turning point of Caesar's or Napoleon's career.

The great attempt of Arnold Toynbee in his interpretation of world history does not escape the error of the axiomaticians. He has been reproached by sociologists for believing in the omnipotence of the scholarly analyst of the laboratory without ever having used the laboratory, and for explaining events as the function of "technical" expressions which hide reality from him in the same manner that the accounts of corporations are carefully edited and kept from the public by so-called "experts." No more convincing, and perhaps funnier, is the position of theosophy, which accepts the all-powerful synarchy, not that of the real elite of technicians, but of "those of the Agarttha" in their Tibetan *sous-sol.*

Let us return to the historians. In Semitic tradition, there is a strong tendency to reduce human history to an aesthetic number structure. The notion of real elite is for this tradition a simple fact of symbolic arithmology.[1] The *turba magna* of the Elect, in the Johannine Apocalypse is gathered up to the ONE by means of numbers: four (the four evangelical animals) and twelve (the twelve judges of the Twelve Tribes, the 144,000 Righteous Ones of Israel). The term *turba magna* itself refers to a people already thus classified, and their classification by number is based on the structure of their hierarchy. Islam, which best preserves the archaic elements of Semitic thought, has elaborated a very complete theory of the real elite, in its "numbered peoples."[2] It is not a case of people accidentally gathered on a *mosalla* (prayer esplanade) for similar gestures or chanting. It refers to a people whose concerted gathering increases until it reaches a collective number ("ordinal," rather than "cardinal," as A. Koyré suggested to the writer in 1932), attaining a Herbartian threshold, with a quantum qualifying it, reversing, as it were, a providential role. Through repetition it consciously announces the "clamor for justice" (*sayha bi'l-Haqq*) of its prophetic animator. For example, we are told that 'Umar was the thirty-eighth among the first forty adherents of Islam who dared to come out of hiding in a provocative manner. And still today, in a Syrian town when the number of initiated Nusayris reaches forty, they can and must found an initiation lodge (forty was also the number of the Martyrs of Sebasteia, who were the protomartyrs of the Greek order of Basilians). It is equally interesting to note that the number 313 is the number of the heroic elite selected by Gideon, and it also happens to be the number of victors in the first raid on Badr by Islam, It is believed that in the supreme holy war the Mahdi will have 313 Companions.

Such symbolic numbers designate not only the simultaneous presence of the members in the group at a given time but also the duration in time of the groupings. According to the Qur'an (18:24), 309 is the number of years of the mysterious slumber of the Seven Sleepers in the Cavern of Ephesus, the time for their maturation by grace. It is also, for the Shi'ites, the period of the exile in hiding of the Fatimite pretenders up to the time of their victorious insurrection with their Mahdi in North Africa.[3]

This quantification of the span of human history would modify the Platonic conception in the *Timaeus*, making the history of the world a homogeneous and indefinite continuum, a simple reflection of the eternal return of the interlocking planetary cycles, with their conjunctions and oppositions. It would introduce into it a singularity, an irreversible progression, with condensations at its critical moments, as individual points on a curve. This would form a fibrous tissue of typical events, in a structure of single or irrational numbers or in series, such as the Fibonacci series (1, 2, 3, 5, 8, 13, 21 . . .). As Bravais showed in constituting the science of phyllotaxy, this series really represents the rhythm of the vital growing of plant stems. The crises of growth, the parturition in pain (ôdînes), of humanity would coincide with the surging of the real elite from the mass in consciously substituting itself for the collective suffering, with the compassion reserved for the "royal souls"; I have noted this point with respect to the fate (and the vow) of Marie Antoinette, the last queen of France.[4]

The strong instinct for unity in Semitic thought is reflected in the undifferentiated character of the Arabic alphabet, which makes of each letter both the sign of a number and the element of a name. The method of aesthetic number is also an onomastic method. The Hegiran year 290, for example, corresponding to the year 902 of our Christian Era, evokes two feminine names of considerable eschatological importance in Islam, Maryam (mother of Jesus: $M + R + Y + M = 290$) and FATIR, the initiation name of Fatima, daughter of the Prophet, ancestress of the Fatimites ($F + A + T + R = 290$). The coincidence of these two values meant for the Fatimite conspirators that the hour had come to revolt, since Maryam was going to "reengender" Jesus for his triumphal return in the form of a Mahdi son of Fatima, in whom the Spirit of Maryam in the Muhammadan cycle is revived. The revolt took place and led in the year 309 of the Hegira to the proclamation of the Fatimite Caliphate, which, incidentally, founded Cairo after Mahdiya.[5]

This instinct persists among non-Semitic peoples in the naming of newborn children. So that something of the elite of their dreams may pass into them, these infants are named after a war hero or a theatrical star, and it is believed that they will survive the rapid decline of their patron's glory, even though nothing of this glory may remain with them. Pierre Janet used to tell us that sociology can attain the real, provided that one applies a little psychological introspection, and this introspection can bring about a vivifying participation in other lives. In order to be conscious of themselves and to realize their destiny, the masses need to turn toward the names of transhistoric personalities, like the names of prophets invoked in the recommandatio animae borrowed from the Essenes by the Church of the Catacombs, a real elite if there ever was one. Frazer, in the "Dying God," and G. Dumézil in his researches on the first kings of Rome, have shown mistakes to which the scorn of this profound instinct can lead men, however basic it may be. And the investigations of parapsychology, like those of Gotthard Booth, have shown how "birds of a feather" gather in constellations of an ideal heaven, yet not without social efficacy.

An elite is necessary for introspection, the true moral relationship of the members to the whole body for the sake of the well-being of the group. In this regard Professor Bendick recently made a very interesting study of real elites in contemporary American society. He found it possible to show the exact bearing of someone emerging from such and such group into institutional life (executive, legislative, and judicial) on styles of dress or art of the different castes. Equally observable was the catharsis effected in these groups by their real elite, which heroically maintains what they consider the right scale of professional values against structural failures.

As a mathematician would say, there is no whole without a structure. In this view the structure precedes the whole, as quantity "fixes" the matter, whether it is a question of space or of time. A social body cannot be studied without introducing the idea of an operational group, or organic factor. It is the real elite which defends it against death. Without the hypothesis of the function of the real elite in such a group, at least latently, this cannot be understood.

But posing this philosophical hypothesis is not enough. We cannot grasp the notion of a real elite without recourse to an observation of human history. For example, there is a number, probably a fixed and limited number — archetypal, Jung would say — to which we can reduce the mass of themes in the universe as they might be catalogued by such folklorists as Aarne-Thompson. This limited number is that of dramatic situations endowed with a viable catharsis in a given social context. The elite becomes aware of these crises and finds in their outcome a recapitulation of its own definitive personality over and above the arbitrary schemes of philosophies of history. It is in such a heroic act that the elite affirms itself; an act endowed with an axial, communicative, and transsocial value, an act which is capable of raising the mass, of giving value to interested acts, as "in a series" (profitable virtues, mercenary acts, mediocre appetites, leprous sins). The heroic elite is linked to these deeds only by its suffering in truly redemptive compassion for the universal.

Here I shall examine just one such act. Let us take the sacrifice of Abraham as an example. As a symbolic archetype this sacrifice has been recapitulated by Muhammad, the founder of Islam. It arises again and again throughout history in nocturnal ascension, found in the Christian sacrifice, the Table of the Sacred Host to console the Apostles for the departure of their Master (1 Cor. 5:1–13). It can also be traced back through the Jewish Passover of the Exodus. It is noteworthy that the mystic Al-Hallaj wanted to become the ritual oblation in such a sacrifice. In assisting at 'Arafat at the dedication of the victim of the annual Hajj, he felt that the popular faith was waiting for the presence of a sole righteous one among the assistants, one whose unreflected intercession might obtain general pardon for all the sins of the year. He wanted to take cognizance of this by compassion; and he was taken at his word.[6]

To which you may say to me: That happened a thousand years ago, are there still analogous cases? Yes, for in a real sense Gandhi was killed for the sake of justice, after a long exalted life, having taken upon himself all the pain and misery of the Hindu people.[7] In the person of this man of pain and suffering these people now recognize themselves. It little matters that after ten years this name should enter a momentary period of silence in India. In other countries, by an apotropaion substitution, the reflection of his torch has lighted other kindred souls. Thanks to the example of this old man grown thin by so many fasts and sacrifices, poised like a flaming target in front of the circle of suffering faces which his fire continues to light and to search out, the spiritual values of man are not defeated by the totalitarianism of nations.

NOTES

1. "L'Arithmologie dans la pensée sémitique primitive," *Archéion* (Rome), July–August 1932, pp. 370–71.

2. "Exposé au Centre International de Synthèse" (Paris, 1932).

3. "Les sept dormants d'Ephèse," *Revue des Études Islamiques,* 1954, pp. 73 f.

4. "Un voeu et un destin: Marie Antoinette, Reine de France," *Lettres Nouvelles,* September–October, 1955, Paris.

5. *La Mubāhala de Médine et l'hyperdulie de Fātima* (Paris, 1955); cf. also "La Notion du voeu et la devotion musulmane à Fātima," extract from *Studi orientalistici in onore di Gioro Levi della Vida* (Rome, 1956), II, 1–25.

6. *Akhbār al-Hallāj* (3d ed.; Paris, 1957), pp. 64, 161–62.

7. "L'Exemplarité de Gandhi," *Esprit* (Paris), January 1955.

PART TWO

Aspects and Perspectives of Islam
(1939)

THE GARDEN AND THE MOSQUE

The garden and the mosque are two closely related ideas in Arabic. In Medina, the mosque where the Prophet is buried is called the *rawda*, that is to say, the garden. Whether it is the Generalife in Granada, the Aguedal in Marrakesh, or the gardens in Cairo, Damascus, Baghdad, or Isfahan, the Muslim conception of a garden impresses us with its consistency: it is essentially a place of reverie in retirement from the world. Even though it may contain the same trees and flowers as ours, this kind of garden contrasts sharply with the classical gardens of the West.

In our classical garden, which began with the Roman Empire and continued with the Medicis and Louis XIV, the intent is to control the world from a central point of view, with long perspective lines leading to the horizon and great water basins reflecting the distances, all framed by relentlessly pruned trees, leading the eye, little by little, to a sense of conquest of the whole surrounding land.

By contrast, the Muslim garden's first and foremost idea is to be enclosed and isolated from the outside world; instead of having its focus of attention on the periphery, it is placed in the center. The garden is created by taking a piece of land, "vivifying" a square section of the desert, into which water is brought. Inside a very high enclosing wall, one finds a staggered arrangement of trees and flowers growing close to one another as one moves from the periphery to the center, and in the center next to a spraying fountain is a kiosk. This garden, contrary to the classical Western garden and the carefully landscaped Japanese garden, enables thought to unfold in an atmosphere of relaxation.

The mosque as the place of public worship by the Muslim community also surprises us by its contrast with the Christian church, even though its builders borrowed the proportioned materials and decorative motifs from the church. The mosque began as an open-air space, usually containing a large central courtyard, but the outer walls of its enclosure were opaque, without the light-diffusing stained glass windows of cathedrals, and one enters it only after passing the ritual ablution basin.

There is a seat of truth, but this movable piece of furniture is relegated to a secondary place; for the faithful, who are massed in parallel ranks like soldiers, must keep their eyes fixed during prayer in a certain direction, that of a small empty central niche, the *qibla*, which marks the direction of Mecca, the place of the propitiatory sacrifice offered to the God of Abraham. Though the wooden doors are often ornate, and the archstones are alternately light and dark, the nave is kept plain and simple. There are no statues acting as intermediary representatives of beauty here below aiming the soul of the worshipper toward the One God, since representation of the human form is forbidden. Only Arabic inscriptions are spread along the walls commemorating the Law in a fixed and solemn way. Finally, instead of a bell tower a minaret rises above from which the human voice surges, replacing the inanimate bronze with the canonical five daily calls to prayer. The whole interest is concentrated voluntarily in this very spare style on the *qibla*, the symbol of the orientation of the heart toward the One.

In buildings other than the mosque – for example, in the civil architecture of the palaces and private homes – the wall decoration is less strictly controlled, but the same principles of style are followed. Muslim artistic decor does not attempt to imitate the Creator in His works by the relief and volume of forms, but evokes Him by His very absense in a delicately suggestive representation that is as perishable as a thin veil, thus underlining simply and with quiet resignation the fleeting passage of things that die—and everything is perishable "except His face." The artist uses material that is malleable, meager, and lacking in thickness: plaster, stucco; and his ornamentation consists of incrustations instead of reliefs. His subjects are geometrical in form but open geometrical forms. They are a reminder, a ponderable representation of a fundamental dogmatic idea attesting that faces and forms do not exist in themselves but are unceasingly recreated by God. We find thus intertwining polygons, circling arcs of varying radii, the so-called *arabesque*, which is essentially a kind of indefinite negation of closed geometrical forms, forbidding us to contemplate, as does Greek philosophy, the inner beauty of a circle, the beauty of a closed polygon like that of a magical and planetary pentacle. Along with the arabesques made of stucco, we find mosaics and carpets when the walls or floors are meant to be covered. These mosaics and carpets express an artistic principle that may be called the blazon principle. There are no graduated nuances moving from one color to the next, but rather colors, five at most, are found in sharp contrast to one another, dull and severe, lacking both transparency and perspective. As with blazons, contrasts are uppermost in importance. The subjects treated in the carpets are either stylized cultivated flowers or hieratized animals. The flowers are not very abundant (there were only five species in fifteenth-century Persia), and there are only three or four kinds of hieratic animals, including the griffin and the phoenix. These are arranged, once again, in arbitrary groupings of colored escutcheons made of decorative particles. There is nothing which better illustrates the theological notion of negating the formal permanence of nature than the doctrine of the blazon with its brutal contrast of colors, its stately metals, and its flowers and "petrified" fantastic animals.

We could discuss in a similar way other aspects of the decorative side of Muslim life, such as the custom that governs greetings and well-wishes, the cut of their clothes, their gold-plated embroideries, and even the seasoning of their meals with contrasting rather than progressive spices. The entire social decor culminates in two higher aspects which lead the mind to either concentrate or relax: style in literature and rhythm in music; two aspects which bring us to the threshold of the book of the holy "recitation" that is chanted throughout the entire Muslim world, the Qur'an.

THE QUR'AN

In order to understand the influence of the Qur'an, written in Arabic and thus making Arabic the language of civilization for hundreds of millions of souls, one must emphasize particular aspects of Arabic grammar, of a Semitic language, for these aspects have determined the style of Qur'anic thought.

By its very structure the Arabic language coagulates and condenses with a metallic hardening, if at times a crystalline brilliance, the idea it wants to express, without bending under the grip of the individual speaking it. Elliptical and gnomic, discontinuous and abrupt, the idea flashes forth from the matrix of the sentence like a spark from flint. Arabic script itself shows us this density: only "the body" of words, the consonants, are noted and are the only ones written in black on a line; whereas "the soul" of words, their vocalization and intonation, are only optionally noted (formerly written in red) but off the line. This physiognomy of condensed contrasts has been imposed by Arabic literature on the rhetoric of all Muslim peoples. The following are a few examples, borrowed from profane and amatory poetry, in which the idea is condensed in contrast with our Aryan languages, in which it would be made more explicit:

"The room where You are has no need of candles" (Ibn al-Mu 'adhdhal).

"Ah! do not fulfill your vow of loving me lest forgetfulness should follow" (Ibn Dawud).

"Think of the Neighbor first, and then of the house (meaning Paradise)" (Rabi'a).

"I wanted to outrun my desire for you, but my desire carried the day" (Mutanabbi).

"Would I call to You thus: 'it is You' if You had said to me: 'it is I'?" (an allusion to the *Fatiha* of the Qur'an) (Hallaj).

If such is the gnomic form of Arabic sentences in the Qur'an, then their psalmody also accentuates the spare and pronounced thinness of early Arabic chant, that of the camel driver, *hadi*. If the melodies in the Christian tradition tended very early toward the "plural" voice by means of polyphony and harmony, the Muslim traditional psalmody preserved the instantaneous consonantal rhythm, whether sonorous or flat, without duration, of percussion instruments, barely colored by the ultracondensed, always monotonous vocalizations.

The text of the Qur'an is presented as a supernatural dictation, recorded by the inspired Prophet, an ordinary messenger responsible for the transmission of this repository. Its literary form has always been considered the highest proof of its personal prophetic inspiration, a miracle of style superior to any physical miracles. The Prophet Muhammad and all Muslims after him venerate in the Qur'an a perfect form of the Divine Word. If Christianity consists fundamentally of the acceptance and imitation of Christ before acceptance of the Bible, Islam, by contrast, consists of acceptance of the Qur'an before imitation of the Prophet. Twenty-five years after the Prophet's death, when the last survivors of his leading Companions, divided by a vendetta, were about to fight each other at a place called Siffin, it was enough for one of the parties to hoist leaves of the Qur'an on the points of their lances to achieve a truce, which led to an arbitration between the Prophet's son-in-law 'Ali and the rival governor of Syria Mu'awiya. The Qur'an is the only intermediary one can invoke with God in order to know His will. The text of its 114 chapters comprising 6,226 verses, intact after 1,300 years (it was accorded an official recension by the third Caliph, 'Uthman, in which the unalterable consonants may be vocalized here and there in different ways), constitutes essentially the revealed code of a supernatural state. A code, for it reminds the faithful of the early covenants made by the Lord with humanity, the fearful Judgment which awaits it, the decree which predestines it, and the sanction which threatens it. In short, along with historical anecdotes, allusions that may come from either the Jewish or the Christian past or may refer to Arab tribal histories or to present political reality, the text introduces unknown prophets and chastizes unbelievers; it also decrees a whole series of social prescriptions, a formula for declaring one's belief in One God, daily ritual prayer, annual fasting, alms tithe, and pilgrimage to Mecca, plus rules governing personal behavior, marriage, and inheritance.

But this book is not only a code. It belongs to that very rare category of book which reveals a perspective on the ultimate purpose of language, which is not simply a commercial tool or an aesthetic toy or a stark windmill of ideas, but which can express a grasp on reality, and which by turning its syntax as a plane does its wings, can "take off" from the ground.

The following verses from the Qur'an enable us to recognize, albeit on a higher level, certain characteristics of Arabic Muslim poetry:

"There is a reminder for one who has a heart and knows to pay heed when he has heard" (50:37).

The structure one must build in one's heart must "be founded on duty to God and not on a precipice that will collapse" (9:109).

At the pilgrimage, "it is not the flesh and blood of victims but the devotion that reaches God" (22:37).

"A word of kindness which forgives is better than an alms-giving which wounds" (2:263).

"The wicked are like captives, mute, deaf, astray, who grope in the glimmers of lightning, who follow a mirage, swimmers who are swallowed up in a dark wave to the point where they do not even see their hand rise from the water" (24:40); "passersby who are seized by an icy wind, their house is as fragile as a spider's web. On the Last Day these wicked persons will ask in vain of the good (such as the wise virgins): 'wait for us, that we may borrow from your light!'" (57:13).

The Qur'an makes parables of the final resurrection out of water that vivifies barren ground, fire struck even from green wood, birds called back by their tamer, each barely etched, just like the lightning.

It should be noted that the Qur'an was the first known Arabic text written not in verse but prose. . . . Rhyme and meter may paralyze thought by demanding strict adherence to mnemotechnic devices. The invention of prose, in this instance, freed thought from metrical demands, caesuras, and cadences. The Qur'an does contain, of course, many passages of rhymed prose, especially in the chronological beginning of its notation, but the rhyme is interrupted when thought demands it and never controls thought. Such is the first original aspect of the Qur'an.

The second is its character of insinuating warning, its call to reflect, as it were, between the lines on a major intention beyond the (minor) voice of the transmitting messenger: hence its character as an "inspired" text. I use this word here just as one says of a journal article "it is inspired," meaning that by a very special technique of the sentence our thought is drawn toward the real author of the article beyond the personality of the one who signs it.

The Idea of the Spirit in Islam
(1945)

The notion of the spirit in Islam is designated, as in other
Semitic langauges, by two sharply contrasting words, *nafs* and
rūh.[1] *Nafs* is the breath of the throat: it comes from the entrails,
it is "carnal" and bound up with the blood, it causes eructation
and spitting and confers the enjoyment of flavor. *Rūh* is the breath
of the nostrils: it comes from the brain, it causes nasal speech
and sneezing (*'ats*, the first sneeze of Adam when God breathed
life into him), it confers the sense of smell and the discernment
of spiritual qualities. Both are discontinuous and rhythmic and
are at the origin of our "internal time" (which is oscillating and
living) as opposed to "astral, cyclic time" (measured by the sun-
dial) and to "gradual time" (measured by the passage of the sand
in the hourglass or by the water clock). *Nafs* is related to *nafth*,
to spit, and to *nafkh*, to breathe into; *rūh* is associated with *rīh*,
to blow.

We shall first examine the experience itself and then take up
the matter of definitions.

The experience of inspiration begins in Islam with the "internal upheavals" felt by Muhammad at the beginning of his
prophetic mission. According to 'Ā'isha, the Prophet of Islam
first had a vision of isolated, luminous letters (several examples
are cited at the head of certain chapters in the Qur'ān) and si-

This essay and the following one are translated by Ralph Manheim and
appear in Joseph Campbell, ed., *The Mystic Vision: Papers from the Eranos
Yearbooks*. Bollingen Series 30, Vol. 6. Copyright © 1983 by Princeton University Press. Excerpts, pp. 315–323, reprinted with permission of Princeton
University Press.

multaneously an audition of isolated sounds; the letters corresponded to the sounds, as with a child learning to spell. Then the Prophet, having learned to spell, was enabled to recite inspired sentences. They were "breathed" into him by the Spirit, *Rūh*, a vague word which can designate the angel as well as God or the Prophet himself.

Beginning with the earliest companions of the Prophet, Muslims made every effort to learn by heart the sacred text of the Qur'ān, which they had heard and read, combining the two breaths *nafs* and *rūh* to produce the rhythm of their recitation: vocalizing and nasalizing (*rūh*) the consonants (*nafs*, which alone are noted in the manuscripts) in a staccato manner, thus designedly polarizing the ambivalent three-letter roots. They hoped to recapture the initial divine breath which had first dictated the sacred text by means of this insinuating, persuasive collective declamation which pierces to the heart. And this is still done in the *dhikr* gatherings of the Muslim orders. W. Haas has given us an excellent description of the *dhikr* of the Kabyle sect, the Rahmānīyah.[2] It is made up of four successive quarter hours of recitation. The disciples are huddled in a circle, crosslegged, forming a chain with their hands; the master stands in the center. For the first eight minutes of each session, the group says *"Allāh"* in a series of violent expirations immediately followed by swifter inspirations producing the sound of a saw. In the second part, likewise of eight minutes, there is a brief inspiration preceding a longer expiration, in the rhythm of forty per minute instead of the preceding sixty. In the middle of the third exercise, however, the rhythm becomes extremely rapid, imposed by the master with the index and middle finger of his raised right hand. At the end of the fourth and last exercise, the disciples kneel around the master in a star-shaped figure, pressing their foreheads to the ground; they are nearly all in a state of trance. The master brings them out of the trance, saying *"Allāh akbar"* and clapping his hands three times. Then they stretch, and a serving brother wipes their faces and kisses them on the head.

(Here I must recall the meeting held on March 10, 1944, by

the Société Asiatique of Paris, at which I discussed some of the statements made by Haas. Haas asserts that the name of God employed is *Hayy* rather than *Allāh* and fails to state whether the expirations were "vomited" from the nose to "empty the brain" or emitted from the pharynx to "empty the entrails.")

And now let us note the different attitudes maintained in the *dhikr* of other orders. The Naqshabandīya blink their eyes, gnash their teeth, and press their tongues against their palates. Historically, the oldest *dhikr* (Hamā'ilī) appears in the twelfth century: blinking eyes, crossed legs, palms on the knees. The breath is emitted under the left breast (to empty the heart); then the word *"Lā"* is expired from the navel (against the sexual demon); then *"Ilāha"* is pronounced on the right shoulder and *"Illa"* at the navel; finally, *"Allāh"* is powerfully articulated in the empty heart. Simnānī (d. 1336) makes slight changes: he "vomits" *"Ilāha"* from the cartilage of his nose, pronounces *"Illa"* on the left side and *"Allāh"* in the heart, keeping the vertebrae of his back and neck "erected" – a painful and purifying constraint. He also holds his right hand over his left hand, in which he clasps his right leg. Henry Maspero here sees a possible Taoist influence (Simnānī had been a Mongol functionary).[3] Indeed, the attitudes and facial expressions of the *dhikr* are in part borrowed and recall the Hindu *asanas*. Sanūsī, in his *Salsabīl*,[4] does not hesitate to classify among the *dhikr* of the Muslim orders the eighty-four poses of the *Jūjīya*, the Yogis, whom Ghawth Hindī (d. 1562)[5] regarded as "Muslims."

The first author who differentiates the names of God used in order to "enter into ecstasy" is Ahmad Ghazālī (d. 1123), in his *Kitāb al-Tajrīd*.[6] The first Sufi who dared to take "poses" in his *dhikr* was Ahmad b. Tarkanshāh Aqsarāyī of Cairo (d. 1330).[7] At the same epoch, Mawlawī Aflakī describes a *dhikr*.[8] But, generally speaking, the accounts of poses in the *dhikr* were not intended to be circulated except among the initiate.

In June 1945 I attended a number of *dhikr* sessions of the Afghan order of the Çishtiya, both at Kabul and at Delhi. These sessions were accompanied by flute playing. The Persian verse which included ecstasy was:

ču resī bekūh Sīnā "arinī" negofte beguzar kih neyarzed īn tamannī
bejawāb "lan taranī"

(If thou mountest to Sinai, say not [to God] "show me [Thy face],"
but pass—for it is not fitting that to such a question thou hearest
the answer "lan taranī" [thou shalt not see me].)

This refers to Moses according to the Qur'ān (7:139).

On the graves of the Turkish sect of the Bayrāmīya, we find
engraved the syllable *Lā* surrounding three little *hā*s (no doubt
vocalized as *hū, hā, hī,* as in the *qādirī dhikr,* i.e., the divine
name *Huwa,* meaning He).

Let us proceed now to the matter of definitions. *Nafs* sig-
nifies in general the carnal soul or animal vitality. *Rūh* is more
mysterious: God, angel, immaterial soul, allusion, spiritual meaning (cf. spirit, "essential perfume" of the flower, according to
the Chinese and according to Boerhaave).[9] *Rūh* establishes communication between man, angel, and God; according to Baqlī,[10]
the angel drinks the tears of penitents and God drinks the tears
of lovers. The colors of the "spirits," discerned in ecstasy, indicate a man's degree of "spiritual finish." In the Nocturnal
Ascension, the soul of the Prophet, rising from the first to the
seventh heaven, divests itself of its seven spiritual coverings,
or *latā'if,* or *'anāsir,*[11] as Ishtar cast off her tunics in descend-
ing to hell. In mystical Islam the soul is composed of concentric spheres. At first only three were counted: from the outside
in, *nafs; qalb,* or *rūh,* seat of the wisdom (*ma'rifa*) which is obtained in dreams; and *sirr,* which is visited by the prophetic
'Aql, and which is the seat of *Tawhīd,* faith in the One God.

In my *Passion,*[12] I have given a list of definitions of the *rūh,*
according to the canonists and theologians of Islam, from Mu-
qātil and Jahm, Mālik, Shāfi'ī and Ibn Hanbal, down to the period when Hellenistic philosophy caused the old thesis that
spirits were "subtle bodies" to be abandoned in favor of the belief (held most strongly since Suhrawardī Maqtūl) that the resurrection was only the liberation of the spirit from servitude to
a corruptible body destined to nothingness.[13] Thus Muslim

writers went from one extreme to the other, from the thesis of the materiality of souls (to explain the torments of the after-life) to that of the pure materiality of the human person.

In Islamic literature the soul, symbolically associated with water and blood, is generally represented by green birds (green-finches) or, more precisely, the souls after death dwell in the gizzards of birds which fly around the throne of God (a very ancient idea).[14] They can be reincarnated without physical copulation if the breath of a saint is breathed into them (the *nefes-oghlu* of the Turkish legends).

And now, in conclusion, I shall cite a list of the chapters of one of the most interesting treatises on the spirit, the *Kitāb al-rūh* by Ibn Qayyim al-Jawzīyah (d. 1350),[15] a Hanbalite canon-ist: Is it permitted to visit the dead in their cemeteries? Meetings with the dead. Does the spirit die? Is it a substance or an accident? Is it tormented in the grave by its sins? Is it, while in the tomb, subject to questions asked by the two angels? Where are the abodes of the spirits, the blessed, the damned? Did souls have existence anterior to bodies? (This the author, contrary to the majority of theologians, denies.) Is the soul threefold (cf. Aristotle) or one? What is the order of the "states" through which it passes in its gradual purification?

NOTES

1. The basic verses of the Qur'ān on *rūh* are 16:87 (and 97:4); 6:98 (*nafs*); 32:8. See L. Massignon, *La Passion d'al-Hosayn-ibn-Mansour al-Hallāj* (Paris, 1922), pp. 482, 517, 596, 661, 689, 852. See also Muhammad A'lā ibn 'Alī al-Tahānawī, *Kashshāf istilāhāt al-funūn, A Dictionary of the Technical Terms Used in the Sciences of the Musulman,* ed. Aloys Sprenger (Calcutta, 1853–62), pp. 540–49 (*rūh*) and 1396–1404 (*nafs*).

2. "Ein Dhikr der Rahmanija," *Der Neue Orient* (Berlin), I (1917), 210–13.

3. Henri Maspero, *Mélanges posthumes sur les religions et l'histoire de la Chine,* II, *Le Taoisme* (Paris, 1950), pp. 107ff. (practiques respi-ratoires); see also Massignon, *Recueil de textes inédits concernant l'his-toire de la mystique en pays d'Islam* (Paris, 1927), pp. 143–45.

4. Muhammad b. 'Alī al-Sanūsī, *al-Salsabīl al-mu'īn fī tarā'iq al-arba'īn:* see Massignon, *Passion,* p. 342; *Recueil de textes,* pp. 169ff.

5. I.e., al-Gawth Muhammad b. Khatīr al-Dīn al-Gujirātī; see Massignon, *Recueil de textes,* p. 169, n. 5.

6. *Recueil de textes,* pp. 95ff.

7. Ibn Hajar al-Asqalānī, *al-Durar al-kāmina fī a'yān al-m'a al-thāmina* (3 vols., Hyderabad, A.H. 1348–55/A.D. 1929–31), I, 16.

8. Ahmad Shams al-Dīn al-Aflakī, *Études d'hagiographie musulmane: Les Saints des derviches tourneurs,* trans. Clement Huart (2 vols., Paris, 1918–22), I, 224.

9. Hermann Boerhaave (1668–1738) wrote extensively on chemistry.

10. Rūzbehān Baqlī: *Recueil de textes,* pp. 113f.

11. 'Alī Husayn Mahfūz, *Al-ibdā'fī madārr al-ibtidā'*(5th ed., Cairo, 1956, *Dār al-kitāb al-'arabī*), p. 320.

12. Above, n. 1.

13. See also my *Recueil de textes,* p. 131 (Ibn Sab'īn).

14. Cf. the poet al-Tirimmāh, *Dīwān* (Beirut, 1900), No. 35, p. 156.

15. Muhammad b. Abī Bakr, called Ibn Qayyim al-Jawzīyah, *Kitāb al-rūh* (3rd ed., Hyderabad, A.H. 1357/A.D. 1938).

Nature in Islamic Thought
(1946)

Last year we examined the notion of "spirit" in Islamic thought. Now I believe it will be worth our while to consider the notion of "nature" in contrast to that of "spirit."

Natura (Greek: φύσις) is traditionally rendered by the Arabic *tabīʿa*. The first Arabic translators of the Syriac translations of the *Organon* used for the word "nature" the word *kiyān*, copied from the Syriac *kyono*, but this term remained rare and was restricted to the innate element in human psychology.

Tabīʿa comes from the root *tbʿ,* to imprint upon a thing, to seal. In the Qurʾān it is used in a rather pejorative sense: a mark of God, the Creator's contempt for His creation, which He imprints with a seal of separation, of shadow, if not of damnation. The "name" which God gives to created things separates them from Him as a "veil" separates things from the light. It is in this sense that the Ismāʿīlīs, the Nusayrīs, and the Drūses call the Prophet Muhammad *Mīm*, the Name (Arabic: *Ism*) and the Veil (Arabic: *Hijāb*).[1] Hallaj said: "God has veiled his creatures with the Name, in order that they may live. . . . if He unveiled his energy to them, they would be destroyed."[2]

The words *tabīʿa* and *tibāʿ* are static, opposed to initiative, movement, will. The first theologians give a negative answer to the question of whether God creates *tabʿān*, that is, "naturally," hence by necessity (which is impossible). It is true that under the influence of the Hellenistic idea of the "immobile prime mover," Muslim theologians ceased to conceive of God's pure act in the form of "movement" (*haraka*), although the profound Semitic tradition of revealed monotheism maintained that

God never ceases to act, to recreate His creation—a Jewish idea reformulated by a great Islamic philosopher, Abū'l-Barakāt al-Baghdādī (d. A.H. 547/A.D. 1153), who showed that the only serious proof of God's existence was this constant actualization, this renewal (*tajaddud*) by which He substantially animates His works.[3]

The first Hellenistic Muslim philosophers are divided into two groups: the "spiritualists," who explain the general functioning and the differentiation of the universe by the action of "spirits" (*ashāb al-rūhāniyīn*), and the "naturists" (*ashāb al-tabā'ī'*), who invoke the action of the four qualities (hot, cold, dry, moist). *Tabā'i',* qualities, also designates by extension the four humors which constitute the living balance of the human body (bile, black bile, blood, phlegm). Under Manichaean influence these qualities and humors came to be considered as "evil," "dark," and the Shī'ite extremists identified them with the souls who were damned for having opposed the proclamation of °Ali as the *khalīfa-imām*—hence predestined elements of Evil.

Two philosophical fables conceived in this period aim in the name of "nature" to minimize the orthodox Muslim belief in the sovereign freedom of God: Ibn al-Rāwandi's fable of the "monotheist Brahmans," who profess that the revelation and the holy scriptures are useless; and the romance of the "Sabaeans," alleged disciples of Hermes, who maintain that through ascetic training human nature, by its own strength and without recourse to revelation, can ascend to the godhead. I have spoken of this in the appendix to Festugière's last book on Greek Hermeticism.[4] This "Sabaean" doctrine is important: it is a spiritual, evolutionist naturism, a spiritualist doctrine of progress.[5] It is also believed that man's natural faculties will enable him to fashion robots and breathe a soul into them. This is the theme of Villiers de l'Isle Adam's famous novel *L'Ève future*.

This spiritualist doctrine of "nature" is close to the Stoic maxim "Ζήν όμολογονένος Τῇ φύσει" in the Arabic Hellenistic texts on natural law, *Nāmūs*. But, by and large, the Muslim thinkers of the third century after the Hijra continued to see a contrast between "nature" and "divine grace." An illustration of this is the title of a famous anonymous manual of Arabic Hellenistic philosophy composed at the time of Caliph Ma'mūn: *Sirr al-khalīqa wasan'at al-tabī'a*,[6] i.e., "The secret of creative grace and the mechanism of nature," in which this mechanism of nature is synthesized by the famous *Emerald Table* (*Tabula smaragdina*) of Hermes, supposedly written by Belinus (Apollonius of Tyana).[7] Another illustration is the first question that Hallaj asks of Junayd: "What enables us to differentiate creative grace (*khalīqa*) from the signs of nature (*'an rusūm al-tab'*)?"[8]

That the spiritualist naturism of that period was a naturism limiting the divine power is proved by the doctrine of talismans bearing the astral "signatures." It is a world order, opposed not only to chance (Greek: τύχη) but to the free intervention of God.

While certain Muslim philosophers, and even the theologian Fakhr Rāzī, attempted to amalgamate the two naturisms, the spiritualist (by astrology) and the materialist (by alchemy), the first Muslim mystics saw in "nature" a mark of punishment inflicted by God on His creatures, an ascetic veil, the sublunar law of pain. 'Amr Makkī attempts to explain the formation of the personality as a disintegration of the "veils" covering the heart, where the divine spark resides, as though incarcerated in a threefold wall.[9] In his Nocturnal Ascension the Prophet successively puts aside the various colored veils (of which there are seven) which conceal the ultimate God from him; these are the human veils. Here we are no longer dealing with the Astral Intellect's Illumination of the human person, but with a suprarational liberation by a transcendent spirit realizing the *Tawhīd*.

These mystics react against the old predestinationist tendency of the *hadīth*s, according to which the Creator, in the very act of creating them, imprints their "nature" upon the two categories of men, the elect and the damned; and the "handful of earth" that contains the elect—*kūnī*, "be!" (using the feminine of *kun*)—is designated as the Light of Muhammad, origin of all the elect.[10]

One should also examine the "sentiment of nature" in Islamic literature; the dominant tendency is a naturism full of resigned serenity. With increasing comprehension comes greater religious satisfaction; and, as Mutanabbi eloquently put it (contrary to the well-known thought of Pascal), "The most pitiful of wretches is he who feels nothing, not he who suffers."[11]

This brings us to a fundamental problem of Semitic, and particularly Jewish, psychology in its most "Kierkegaardian" aspect: there is a hidden but divine good in suffering, and this is the mystery of anguish, the foundation of human nature. Our nature does not bear the mark of anguish outwardly as a temporary damnation or sanction; it assimilates it inwardly, like a void into which the divine presence rushes in all its glory. Whatever may be said on this matter, many Muslim thinkers have been struck by this notion of the primordial anguish of created nature given to man in his existential, eschatological, finalist actuality – this "adventure," the presentiment of which sublimates the "nature" in us. Some years ago a highly interesting argument on this subject occurred in Cairo between André Gide and the Muslim writer Taha Husayn, in connection with Gide's novel *Strait Is the Gate*.[12] The Muslim replied triumphantly that Islam had also known anguish: not only had it contributed to the elaboration of a theory of chivalric love, the love of ideal renunciation, in the Middle Ages, but it had also inspired the pseudo-blasphemies of the great blind [Syrian] poet, Ma'arrī.

NOTES

1. Anonymous Nusayri, MS Pers. 1934, fol. 81 b.

2. Al-Hallāj, *Akhbār al-Hallāj, texte ancien relatif à la prédication et au supplice du mystique Musulman al-Hosayn b. Mansour al-Hallāj*, ed. and trans. Louis Massignon and Paul Kraus (Paris, 1936), p. 112 (text), p. 50 (introduction).

3. Abū'l-Barakāt al-Baghdādī, *Al-mu'tabar fī'l-hikma* (Hyderabad, Dā'irat al-Ma'ārif, A.H. 1357/A.D. 1938) cites Ibn Taymīya, *Minhāj*, I, 93, 99, 112, 118, and Ibn Abī'l-Hadīd, *Sharh al-nahj*, I, 297.

4. André-Jean Festugière, *La Révélation d'Hermès Trismégiste* (4 vols., Paris, 1944–), Appendix, I, 384ff.

5. See P. Kraus, *Jābir ibn Hayyān al-Tarasūsī, Essai sur l'histoire des idées scientifiques dans l'Islam* (Paris, 1935); idem, *Jābir b. Hayyān. Contribution à l'histoire des idées scientifiques dans l'Islam* (2 vols., Cairo, 1942–43); idem in *Rivista degli studi orientali* (Rome), XIV (1934).

6. MS. Ar. Paris 2302, studied by H. S. Nyberg; see his *Kleinere Schriften des Ibn al-ʿArabī* (Leyden, 1919) under A III, pp. 38–44.

7. Julius Ruska, *Tabula Smaragdina, Ein Beitrag zur Geschichte der hermetischen Literatur* (Heidelberg, 1926).

8. See above, n. 2.

9. ʿAlī b. ʿUthmān al-Hujwīrī, *The Kashf al-Mahjūb, the Oldest Persian Treatise on Sufism*, trans. R. A. Nicholson (London and Leyden, 1911), p. 309.

10. Mustafā Yūsuf Salām al-Shādhilī, *Majmūʿat Jawāhir al-ittilāʿ wa-durar al-intifāʿ ʿalā matn Abī Shujāʿ* (Cairo, A.H. 1350/A.D. 1931), p. 123 (*qabda maʿlūma* = *kūnī* of the Carmathians).

11. Al-Mutanabbī, *Dīwān* (Beirut, 1900); cf. Blaise Pascal, *Pensées*, ed. Leon Brunschvicg (3 vols., Paris, 1904), No. 399: "On n'est pas misérable sans sentiment: une maison ruinée ne l'est pas; il n'y a que l'homme de misérable: *Ego vir videns.*"

12. Taha Husayn, *al-ʿUsūl wa-l-ghāyāt*, in *al-Mahrajān al-alfīya li-dhikr Abī-l-Aʿlā al-Maʿarrī* (*al-Majmaʿ al-ʿilmi al-ʿarabī*), (Damascus, 1945), pp. 19ff.

Time in Islamic Thought
(1952)

Since Kant, mathematics has accustomed us to consider time as an *a priori* form of our intuition; joined to three-dimensional space, time constitutes the fourth dimension of an expanding universe. Nevertheless, we feel a kind of contraction in our thinking when it aspires to apprehend time; we feel that the possible exceeds the existential,[1] that the data of the problem go beyond the solutions, that the quest surpasses the findings. Minkowski's "time as a fourth dimension" remains open to discussion.

A religious thought wholly oriented toward a transcendent monotheism, such as Islam, has an entirely different vision of time. There is no question here of inventing time; it is time that reveals to us the order (*amr*) of God, the fiat (*kun, kūnī*), which releases the acts we perform as responsible beings. Thus for the Muslim theologian time is not a continuous "duration," but a constellation, a "galaxy" of instants (and similarly there is no space, but only points). The heresiographers condemn as materialists the "Dahriyūn," the philosophers who divinize Duration (*dahr*).

For Islam, which is occasionalist, and apprehends the divine causality only in its actual "efficacy," there exists only the instant, *hīn* (Qur'ān 21:111; 26:218; 37:174, 178), *an* (Q. 16:22), the "twinkling of an eye" (Q. 16:79: *lamh al-basar*), the laconic

Translated by Ralph Manheim. This essay appears in Joseph Campbell, ed., *Man and Time: Papers from the Eranos Yearbooks.* Bollingen Series 30, Vol. 3. Copyright © 1957 Princeton University Press. Excerpts, pp. 108–114, reprinted with permission of Princeton University Press.

announcement of a judicial decision of God, conferring on our nascent act His decree (*hukm*), which will be proclaimed on the day when the cry of Justice (Q. 50:41) is heard.

This discontinuous perception of time in "instants" is not pure religious subjectivity. The instant appears to the entire Muslim community as an authoritative reminder of the Law, as inevitable as it is unexpected. The fundamental instant in the life of Islam appears at nightfall with the new moon, *ghurrat al-hilāl*, which declares "open" a period of variable duration for the liturgical accomplishment of various legal observances (pilgrimage, period of widowhood, etc.).[2] It is not permissible to foresee the new moon by means of theoretical tables; it must be watched for and established by two "witnesses of the instant." This method is still observed by all Islam (except for the Ismailians). It is the *iltimās al-hilāl*. In this Islam accords with the most primitive peoples of mankind, who, in the very irregularity of the phases of the moon, revere the manifestation of a mysterious Will independent of the solar seasons.[3] The most that Islam tolerates is a very primitive calendar, consisting in the twenty-eight lunar mansions (364 days), furnishing empirically the name of the star (*Najm*), or rather of the zodiacal constellation, in which the rising of the new moon must be watched for at the end of each lunar month. This instant, at nightfall, marks the beginning of a day, *yawm*, which establishes an indiction or *epoche*, the beginning of an era: such as July 16, A.D. 622, the first day of the Muslim hegira to Medina; or such as, in earlier times, the "*ayyām al-'Arab*," the tribal battles that constituted the only real calendar of the Arabs before Islam. These are "stopping places" for the minds of men, implying "introversion" into the memory.

But the only perfect, self-sufficient instant is the Hour (*Sā'a*), the hour of the Last Judgment, the final summation of the decrees of all responsibilities incurred; this Hour must be awaited with a sacred awe (Q. 42:17), for the "witness of this instant" is the divine Judge (according to the Shi'ites and the Sufis, all instants from those of the Five Prayers to the Stations of the Pilgrimage can be personified in their Witnesses). This Ultimate

Day (*yawm akhīr*) is preceded by other premonitory "catastrophic days" (*yawm 'asīb, wāqi'a,* etc.), whose aspects are described in the apocalyptic collections (King Abdullah of Jordan, recently assassinated, read me one of them one evening two years ago at Amman);[4] the Ultimate Day is their culmination and conclusion.

All the other "days" are imperfect, insufficient to themselves; for the decree they proclaim is fulfilled only after a delay (*imhāl*), at the end of a certain period (*labath:* Q. 18:24;[5] 20:42). It is actually through this idea of a "period" that the notion of "duration" was introduced obliquely into Islamic thought; here "duration" is the silent interval between two divine instants, the announcement and the sanction; it is this variable period that the responsible man must utilize for expiation in order to conjure the sanction (which remains inevitable); it is the "sounding board" between the two sonorous "instants."

In the Qur'ān the second "instant," that of the sanction, is called the term (*ajal*), or more precisely the marked term (*ajal musammā*). This was one of the first theological notions to be studied in Islam, in connection with the "decree" concerning a murdered man. Did he die at the "term marked" by God? Should God not bring him back to life *before* the Universal Judgment in order to "pay" him publicly the "price of his blood" at the expense of his murderer? This is what the Qur'ān teaches through the Return of Jesus and the Awakening of the Seven Sleepers of Ephesus; the *Raj'a*, as the Shi'ites call it, the Return for the Vengeance of Justice, which is not yet the Resurrection but its prodrome: the rising of eschatological time which "accelerates" (*tajaddud*) the process of decomposition of a world of corruption.

Thus the first Muslim thought knows nothing of continuous duration and considers only atoms of time, "instants," *ānāt* (pl. of *ān*), *awqāt* (pl. of *waqt:* cf. Q. 15:38). They are not "states." Arabic grammar does not conceive of "verbal times" [tenses] as states; in principle it knows only "verbal aspects," the finished [perfect] (*mādī*) and the unfinished [imperfect] (*mudāri*) which mark, outside of our time, the degree in which the (divine) action has been made real. But little by little, particularly in the spoken language, Arabic grammar has come to consider verbal time in relation to the responsible agent, that is, present, past, and future. It applies the term "*ḥāl*" (modality) to the subjective consciousness that we form of the instant surrounded by the "halo" of beauty (cf. Jullabi, 369) that it evokes for us.[6] This *ḥāl* is not strictly speaking a state. The primitive mystics (among them Junayd), as we shall see, regard it as an instant without duration, colored by a fugitive virtue. Let us consider, rather, the grammatical analyses of the instant (*waqt*): according to Qushayrī (*risāla* 37) the phrase "I come at dawn" marks an instant, because it announces an imagined event (*ḥādith mawhūm*) by means of a verifiable event (*ḥādith mutaḥaqqiq*). In the analyses of a later theologian, Fakhr Rāzī, who with Aristotle regards time (*zamān*) as an instant that elapses (*ān sayyāl*), (*mabaḥith mashr.*, I, 647), the same phrase announces a well-known recurrence (*mutajaddid ma'lūm:* at dawn) in order to date another, imagined recurrence (*mutajaddid mawhūm:* "I come" = simple possibility). Jurjani was to revive this second definition (*sh. mawāq.*, 219, *istil.* 119).

First of all we observe that although Qushayrī and Fakhr Razi are both predestinarians, Qushayrī places the accent on the realization of the believer's hope through mysterious divine omnipotence;[7] whereas the very Hellenized Fakhr Razi has recourse to a knowledge of the laws (recurrence) of nature, contingent or otherwise. Possibly Qushayrī still believed, like his predecessor Ibn al-Qāss (d. 945), that the sun's movement is discontinuous, that it has each night a resting place (*mustaqarr:* Q. 36:38; 18:84), which it leaves only at divine order.

Secondly the word *mutajaddid* in Fakhr Rāzī is highly interesting; it is an attenuating Hellenization of the word *tajaddudāt* (innovations) conceived by his adversaries, the Karrāmiya, and by Abū'l-Barakāt, in order to stress (in opposition to the Greeks) the idea that God is interested in particulars, and that He excites our free acts by His grace; and in order to inject into the divine Essence (as Will to create our acts) an infinity of modalizations of His "fiat," corresponding to each of the instants in which He makes us responsible for new acts (*ihdāth fī'l Dhāt*).[8] Abū'l-Barakāt even believed that these modalizations or innovations in the divine Essence constitute the only real proofs of God's existence. For him then there was an *ordinal* plurality of events in God; and for this reason he wrote that "time is the dimension of Existence" (*al-zamān miqdār al-Wujūd;* cf. Q. 32:4 for *"miqdār"*). Whereas like a good scholastic Fakhr Rāzī admitted only a *cardinal* plurality in God, relating to the ideas of His Knowledge "which creates things." And this leads him, according to Ghazālī (*mi'yār,* 172, *maqāsid*), to the Aristotelian definition of time as "the number of movement according to the before and after" (*Physics,* IV, 11, 219b, 1–2).

Tempted by Neoplatonism, the later mystics of "existential monism" (as opposed to the "testimonial monism" of the primitives) returned to the Platonic notion of a divine Duration: Jurjani said: *"al-dahr imtidād al-Hadrat al-ilāhiya"*–"Duration is the expansion of the Divine Presence" (*ist.* 111). Plato (followed by Crescas in the fourteenth century) saw "Chronos" as a cyclical movement of the Uppermost Heaven, a living and numbered reflection of intelligible Eternity.

The later mystics adapted three very ancient Arabic technical terms to this notion of divine duration: *sarmad,* the absolutely fixed (opp. *dahr,* the fixed in relation to change); *azal,* the pre-eternal; *abad,* post-eternity. Hallāj, however, said that *azal* and *abad* are mere embryos from the standpoint of the *yaqīn* (the instant of divine certainty perceived in the heart).

In seeking to determine the essential Muslim idea of time, it seems most profitable to turn away from the theorists' oscillations between Platonic "duration" and Aristotelian "number of movement," and to consult the experimental testimony of the "practitioners": grammarians and fundamentalists (in canon law), physicians, psychologists of ecstasy, and musicians.

The grammarians, we recall, use the term *hāl* for the time

that is "subjective" relative to the agent, to the "now" to which it testifies immediately; this instant is without duration; for when retrospective allusion is made to it by means of the historical present (*'alā'l-hikāya*: according to the narrative mode), the allusion is powerless to revive this "now."

Beginning with Shāfi'ī, the fundamentalists, who use the methods of the syntaxists (*sarfiyūn*) but do not yet resort to Stoic (or Aristotelian) logic, apply to the *hāl* principle of the *ta'mīn al-hukm*, the generalization of a decree (in the domain of its legitimacy); this is the *istishāb al-hāl* (extremely limited among the Hanbalites), a kind of tacit renewal of the status quo, i.e., to perpetuate (*ibqā*) the momentary description (*wasf*: a Kharijite word, hence having a Qadarite flavor) of a juridical case observed, so that it could legitimately apply to other analogous cases the canonical decree (*hukm*) that has been attributed to it. — This is an implicit recourse to a kind of conceptualism, substituting for the "description" (*wasf*) a "quality" (*sifa*), an "idea" susceptible of logical universality (*kulliya*) to the extent compatible with the data revealed (cf. the very strange arithmetic of the division of inheritances according to the Qur'ān. — Nevertheless, this is a kind of virtual, immaterial duration, which leads Islam to admit that everlasting spiritual substances can exist "outside" of God (angels, souls).

Rāzī, the great physician, who was a *Dahrī*, a partisan of the eternal Duration of the universe, denied any duration to psychic phenomena such as pleasure (*ladhdha*); in a special work he affirmed clinically that pleasure is a state *without* duration; for it is simply the threshold of convalescence, the passage between sickness and health. Thus the religions are wrong in speaking of "eternal bliss."

The first psychologists of ecstasy, *wajd*, gave it this name to signify a sudden shock of grace, perceived as an instant of anguish (*wajada* = to find; *wajida* = to suffer), without duration but endowed with a variety of mental colors (joy, sorrow; gratitude, patience; dilation, constriction; etc.).[9] The first mystics denied these states (*ahwāl*, pl. of *hāl*) any real duration; then Muhāsibī, taking a step very like that of the fundamentalist Shāfi'ī, gave the *hāl* a virtual, ideal "duration"; and Ibn 'Atā' maintained that after interruption, a "resumption" of the *ḥāl* was possible (*'awd:* contra Junayd);[10] that it remained the same. Thus the disappearance of the instant of anguish could leave the heart with a kind of "rhythmic impulse" and an enduring promise of plenitude, the beginning of a Wisdom situated outside of time. "What is the instant?" Hallāj was asked. – "It is a breeze of joy (*farja*) blown by pain – and Wisdom is waves which submerge, rise, and fall, so that the *instant* of the Sage is black and obscured" (Kalābādhī, No. 52). He also said: "The instant is a pearl-bearing shell, sealed at the bottom of the ocean of a human heart; tomorrow, at the rising tide of Judgment, all the shells will be cast on the beach; and we shall see if any pearl emerges from them" ('Attār, *Tadhkirat al-Awliyā'*).

Thus the instant of anguish can in some sense survive, but like a germ of hidden immortality, buried at the bottom the heart (*tadmīn*), not like those virtues worshiped by certain fanatical ascetics, who, through wishing to keep them as emblems, forsake for them the God who made them desire them. We can form an idea of this "hidden" persistence if we recall that the duality of the *annunciatory instant* is not symmetrical, but oriented toward the future, toward the marked term (*ajal musammā*) that has been "announced" to us, and that the "empty" dimensions of the period of this expectation engender a kind of spiritual rhythm destined to impress on each creature its personal melodic mark in the symphony of the Beyond.

Starting with the (wooden) percussion instruments, the Muslim musicians, the "practitioners," produce the rhythm (*īqā'*) by differentiating the *dīh* (dull blow on the *edge* of the darabukka) from the *tā'* (sonorous stroke on the *center*); the irregularity in the alternation of these two strokes (*naqra*) creates a rhythmical movement, a dance (left foot, right foot). The systems of silences (*sukūn*), broken by such alternating strokes to form distinct rhythmic patterns (*mas, mūdī, murabba',* etc.), elevate us beyond the phonetics of noises toward a phonology of sounds, toward a consideration of the structure of immaterial harmonies.

Similarly, the ambivalence of the instant of anguish, understood as an otherness oriented toward its "marked term," makes us transcend it; leading us to that finality (*nihāya*), that "piercing through," which is more than our original "rising up" (*bidāya*); for as Hallāj remarked, it is the "Realization" (*tahqīq*). The instant of anguish (*yawm al-hasra*, Q. 19:40) is essentially prophetic — it does not scan the passage of time in linear fashion as the Aristotelian water clock does, nor does it periodically invert the many-phased cycles of astral time, caused by the "fall of Psyche," as the hemispherical gnomon of the Chaldeans does; rather, it announces the final stopping of the pendulum of our vital pulse on the tonic of its scale, on the "place of its salvation" (St. Augustine). It is not a fragment of duration, it is beyond doubt a divine "touch" of theological hope, which transfigures our memory forever.

NOTES

1. Leibniz' dictum, borrowed from Ghazālī: "there is nothing more in the possibles [*imkān*] than what exists."

2. That is why the liturgical twenty-four-hour day is a nychthemeron.

3. Cf. the rejoicing at the full moon of the Passover in Israel (= the coming of the Messiah).

4. This was a Shi'ite Apocalypse in which Ja'far Sādiq advised Nafs Zakiya against rising up on behalf of justice, before the Hour. [King Abdullah was assassinated July 20, 1951. – Ed.]

5. The 309 years of "sanctifying" slumber of the Seven Sleepers. The twelve lunar months (*ahilla*, pl. of *hilāl*; Q. 2:185; 9:38), composing the Hegirian year (*sana*) on the *ajal*; cf. the Shi'ite Mufid; and the word *husbān* (Q. 18:37).

6. The "*hāl*" taken as a proper name: "Yahya" (= he lives = John), "Yamūt" (he dies), "Yazūl" (he passes).

7. The recurrence that is an appointment, *mī'ād* (Q. 28:85; 34:29). – The incidence (*hulūl*) of the accident of inflection, the infusion of grace.

8. Cf. Ibn Abī'l-Hadid, *Sharh Nahj al-balāgha;* Ibn Taymiya, *Minhāj, al-sunna,* whence the problem: Is what is not foreseen by the Law *licit a priori* (*barā'a aslīya, ibāha*)? On the *hikāya*, cf. the *ta'līq* and the *af'āl qalbiya*.

9. Shāfi'ī was first to posit the permanence of the *wujūd*, of a status quo, an intelligible qualification.

10. On this '*awd*, cf. *ta'arruf*, 96.

Salman Pak and the
Spiritual Beginnings of Iranian Islam
(1934)

Introduction: Mada'in and Kufa;
How to Approach the Study of Salman

On the east bank of the Tigris River, in one of the loops of its meanderings, below Baghdad, springs forth in a single thrust thirty meters high the only vault left standing of the palace of Ctesiphon, a millennial capital, heir of Babylon. It is the Taq-e Kisra, "the vaulted arch of Khosrow," and curled at his feet, to the northwest, one ends by discovering after the small town of Hudhayfa the small tomb of Salman the Pure, Salman Pak. A German expedition undertook an excavation of this field of ruins; I skirted it three times, in 1907, 1908, and 1927. Surprised by the historical contrast of these two monuments, the high vault and the hidden tomb, I became engaged in research concerning the legend and the real personality of Salman. I would like to present today the general orientation of this research as well as to describe the first findings from it.*

*Presented May 30, 1933, at a conference of the Société des Études Iraniennes (Musée Guimet, Paris). Abridged version here. Omitted also from this essay for this volume is most of the scholarly apparatus, including appendices of unpublished texts and analysis of primary sources and their classification with lists of oral and written transmitters and documents, lists of works in oriental and European languages, 207 footnotes, and diacritical marks on Arabic and Persian words, etc. All the above are included in *Opera Minora* I, 443–83, which is available in most major American libraries for specialists or students specializing in Islamic history and civilization.

The two sister cities, Ctesiphon to the east, Seleucia to the west, which two thousand years ago followed here the Chaldean cities of Upi and Akshak, bear in the history of Islam the single name Mada'in.

It was the capital of all the Persian Orient; it was as great in civilization as its Byzantine rival, Constantinople, which Islam was not to capture for eight more centuries. Like it and like Rome, Mada'in had seven market towns, to the west, Darzijan, Bahrasir, Jundishapur (Koke, toward Muzlam Sabat) rejoining the Nahr al-Malik; to the east, Asfanabr, Rumiya, and probably Nuniyafadh and Kurdafadh. It was the sole bridgehead toward Persia and the Asian highlands, the administrative center of the Sassanid Empire, home of the classical Pahlavi language, religious center of Nestorian and Manichaean patriarchies, of the Jewish exilarchate, capital of the oriental bank and of oriental science. Coins struck there bore the simple imprint "Baba," or *"al-Bab,"* that is to say "the threshold," just as following it Istanbul was to be the Ottoman "Sublime Port," and as before it Babylon, its ancestry destroyed, had been "Babel," "the Door (of God)."

Likewise, Mada'in became for its Arab conquerers, remaining faithful to the natal climate and entrenched in their camp of Kufa at the edge of the desert, the "threshold" of Persian splendors. It was to take more than one hundred years, with the foundation of Baghdad, for Mada'in to decline. While waiting, it nourished Kufa, not only with its treasures and its harvests, but with its trades and its modes of thought which it communicated to the Arab clans of Kufa by introducing their Iranian "clients" who had become Muslims there, and Salman, the first Persian to come to Arab Islam, would return to die in Mada'in, where his humble tomb reminds the Shi'ite pilgrims who go there to pray of his double destiny, symbolically the precursor and spiritual initiator of "the threshold," *"al-Bab,"* which his fidelity as a friend earned him in nascent Islam: "May I live and die, faithful friend, like you . . . who has not betrayed."

The history of the first century of the Hegira is still only imperfectly established; the chronological outline presents several contradictions, especially in the years 36–37, which the lack of independent foreign sources does not help us to resolve. And when one moves on to the study of the biographies, as is the case here for Salman, they turn to dust in our hands, like the dune into tiny grains of sand. They are only detached, atomized anecdotes from the hadith (or accounts) attributed to such and such a direct witness by a "chain," more or less sure, of intermediaries. Their tenor, beneath their naive appearances, most often conceals intentional distortions and folkloric borrowings in which, as Wellhausen has observed, we hardly have a constant criterion to follow (when one no longer has as guide a principal source whose degree of credibility has been established) and are forced to resort to certain indirect methods of approximation.

Wellhausen, Goldziher, and Lammens have thus taken advantage of the geographical distribution of hadith between the Medinan, Iraqi, and Syrian schools, measuring the degree of credibility of each one according to the political significance for them of the events which they describe to us. Caetani, Levi della Vida, and Buhl have, with personal nuances, applied the same method.

This geographical distribution of hadith suggested by Ibn Sa‘d seems to require a subdivision for the Iraqi school: Basra very early on became differentiated from Kufa. As for the political distribution between hadith favorable to the Umayyads and hadith favorable to the Alids, which are only of global and undifferentiated value for the course of a century (37–132 A.H.), recourse to the heresiographical examination of hadith permits one to perceive therein some of the developments, thanks to a distribution among Sunni hadith (at first *murji'i*), Zaydi hadith, and that of other Imami sects. These three categories are completely different; the Sunni hadith do not cease to become enriched, almost unconsciously, even after the third century, with foreign elements; whereas the Zaydi hadith and especially the Imami hadith close their collections beginning with the first generation of their founders. They are "closed"; they provide therefore a *terminus ad quem* for their common hadith, and a *terminus a quo* for certain of their own hadith: we shall see this for those which concern Salman.

For the Iraqi school of Kufa, which interests us most here and which includes all the Zaydi and Imami scholars of tradition, one can go back still further than the period attained thanks to the heresiographical criterion and rejoin the primitive period of supremacy of the *buyutat al-'Arab* in the misr (camp) of this turbulent jund (army) (14–37 A.H.). By classifying the rawis (transmitters) according to their clans and their tribal alliances (*ahlaf*) which Islam could not later extirpate and in which the clientele of the *mawali* was molded at the beginning, we have been able to extract the role of the Abdalqays in the biography of Salman.

In our opinion, the legend of Salman contains archaic elements which the study of the heresies on one hand and of the tribal alliances on the other hand permits us to isolate and to date—invalidating on several points the excessive criticism of Horovitz and tending to confirm the historicity of the person of Salman.

Summary of the Classical Biography: Exposition and Examination of the Critical Theory of Horovitz

The classical tradition, common to Sunnism and Shi'ism, classified the Persian Salman among the principal Companions of the Prophet, in a separate category. He is one of the three non-Arabs (*sabiqun*) first converted, along with the Greek Suhayb and the Abyssinian Bilal, and the traditional physiognomy of this "foreigner" (*'ajami*) presents particularly prominent traits.

Born in Persia and, while still young, led to Christianity by a pronounced ascetic vocation, he went from master to master and from city to city, exposing himself to exile and to slavery, not only in order to find a stricter rule of life and the rigorous monotheism sought after by the other Hanifa [pre-Islamic ascetics], but in order to join a Messenger of God, who had been described to him and whom he finally found in Muhammad. Admitted into his circle of intimates, Salman counseled him at the Battle of the Trench, and after his death was the faithful friend of his family, that is to say of the Alids, and the defender of their legitimate and misunderstood rights, until his death in Mesopotamia in Mada'in.

At first glance, the documentation of this life appears heterogeneous. First, there is a long continuous account, autobiographical, a prologue, on the history of his conversion. Then, for the rest of his life, rare and scattered landmarks around the two essential affirmations, the intimate relationship with the family of the Prophet (hadith: *minna Ahl al Bayt*) and the political defense of their legitimacy (saying: *"kardid o nakardid"*). Upon taking a closer look, other difficulties appear, already raised by several Muslim authors, especially Shi'ites, who proposed solutions which are a bit too concordant. From 1909–13, on the other hand, Clement Huart, publishing three accounts of the "prologue," decided it was nonhistorical, but defended the authenticity of Salman at the Battle of the Trench. In 1922, in a sober, dense, and incisive monograph, Horovitz undertook to demonstrate that the legend of Salman was only a myth, born of an etymological investigation, bearing precisely on the word "Trench" (*khandaq*). He proceeded to adhere to the theory which, with Max Mueller, traces the origin of a myth to a "malady of language." According to him, a simple name, "Salman," appeared first in the imprecise lists which Muslim apologetics was trying to draw up of the *"kitabiyun* witnesses," Jews and Christians who paid homage to the mission of the Prophet as it was beginning to unfold. This name, vaguely attributed to a Persian, served to embellish the account of the Battle of the Trench (*khandaq*). The word *khandaq*, long since Arabized but of Iranian origin and signifying a strategic work of supposed Persian origin, led to the idea of making this Salman "Farisi," of whom nothing was known, a Persian engineer, a converted ex-Mazdean, an intimate counselor of Muhammad, and by that alone deserving to be inscribed on the Shi'ite list of the first defenders of the Alids. Beginning with this hypothesis, Horovitz sees in the other biographical data concerning Salman only the consequences of this etymological myth. If he is mentioned among the participants in the rite of brotherhood, it is in order to consolidate his existence as *sahabi* (companion of the Prophet) if he is pointed out among the combatants of Iraq, at Qadisiya, Mada'in, Kufa, and Balanjar, it is due to his Persian characteristics. As for his alleged intimacy with the family of the Prophet, his adoption attested to by the amount of his pension under 'Umar, and his intervention in favor of 'Ali in the year 11, these are Shi'ite additions to the initial etymological theme. Nothing exists therefore with certainty in this biography other than the name "Salman," an Arabic word, moreover, a known first name, for which a *kunya* [Abu 'Abdallah] had first been invented (without the inventor's dreaming that a *mawla* (Persian convert client of an Arab Muslim) perhaps did not have the right to do so) and then, later, a Persian first name was added. It is the imagination of Persian converts to Islam which is responsible for all this artifice of made-up details.

Let us first of all raise some general objections to the findings of this nominalist historical critique:

1. The mythical, or—still better—gnostic, interpretation of a personality does not substitute a posthumous and unreal phantom for an authentic human fact; it expresses a social need for a total explanation, a reaction which is often almost immediate, contemporary with the human fact which provokes it; and the paradoxical transformation which it attempts through this is not *a priori* illegitimate or unacceptable.

2. An etymological myth could arise in a given civilization only at a certain stage of grammatical development, and that of Salman appeared formed, in Arab Islam, prior to this stage.

3. It is true that the legend of Salman was amplified and conserved especially due to the devotion of Iranian Muslims, but it is in Arabic that it was first constituted and defined, at Kufa. And it is because the memory of this Persian client of the Prophet persisted that it became imposed, little by little, into popular Iranian devotion; it is not through a subconscious

desire for racist revenge on the part of the newly Islamicized Persians that the character of Salman was invented.

Let us move on to the details.

The critique of Horovitz could not make us revise, and with reason, the fundamental heterogeneity of the coupling of "Salman and al Farisi": with an Arabic first name (with Aramaic overtones) coupled with an Iranian ethnic extraction, it has a strangeness too evident to have been forged so early.

While the other "witnesses," *kitabiyun* or not, which tradition groups around the Prophet — Bahira-Sergios, Tamim Dari, and others — are only silhouettes, unreachable and suspect, we have at least two solid chains of authority which preserve the physiognomy of Salman in the historical cadre of the *Mushajarat* [disputes among the *sahaba* or companions of the Prophet]: (1) the high antiquity of the discussions between Shi'ite sects at Kufa concerning his religious role in relation to the Prophet and to 'Ali; and (2) the attempt at doubling his personality between a "Salman Juhani Isfahani," a Sunni rawi of the school of Medina, and the Salman (Qurazi Isfahani) who was an intimate of the Shi'ism of the school of Kufa and Mada'in. Let us include here, lest it be forgotten, the reclamations made since the beginning of the third century of the Hegira by those who claim to be descendants of the brother or the daughters of Salman and the long-established custom of pilgrimage to his tomb in Mada'in.

On several points of detail, on the other hand, the criticism of Horovitz seems convincing; we shall encounter them later.

Ivanow, to whom we owe the knowledge of the *Umm al-Kitab*, wherein the gnostic legend of Salman occupies such an important place, has taken up (in an independent fashion) the hypothesis of Horovitz concerning the Iranian coloration of this legend under a more admissible and more nuanced form. It is no longer a question of initial invention, but of retouches, no longer racist, but religious, of Manichaean origin.

Let us clarify that. It is not possible to attribute to an Iranian cultural influence the invention even of the type of Salman, at Kufa, where the names of the streets underwent the beginnings of Iranization only in 132 A.H., at the time of the conquest by the Khurasanian army of the Abbasids, and where the two insurrections of the *mawali* (plural of *mawla*), in 43 A.H. and in 67 A.H., had an Arab framework. (It must not be forgotten that the Persian language was reborn in a literary form, thanks to the *shu'ubiya*, only in the 3rd/10th century.) But the conversion of the Hamras, Persian garrisons (already Arabized in Hira and the Yemen), in 14–17 A.H., their installation in Kufa, Basra (and probably Mada'in), and their reinforcement by half-breeds, sons of Persian captives taken at 'Ayn al-Tamr and Jalula (from 12 to 17 A.H.), when they became adults, formed a hybrid milieu, especially in Kufa. There, upon contact with nascent Islam renewing Abrahamic monotheism, as in older days upon contact with nascent Christianity in Galilee, an intellectual effervescence was produced, that which is called gnosis. Samaritan and Greek in Christianity, gnosis was Manichaean in origin, that is to say Aramaic and Iranian in Islam. In both cases it is not a question of rational conciliation between the philosophy of the sciences and a theology, a later thing, but the ardent acceptance of a new and supernatural faith in the milieu of an older culture, which, in light of its new belief, contemplates the visible universe through a prism illuminated by ancient myths.

We are not concerned here with sketching the formation of this Muslim gnosis nor with its exposition, whatever fundamental role was played by Shi'ism therein, or whatever tacit borrowings Sunnism drew from it, from the *'aql awwal* to the *nur muhammadiyyah*. We wish simply to affirm, with Ivanow, that a little of the physiognomy of Khurmuzta, the Primordial Man of the oriental Manichaeans, was projected onto that of the historical Salman, in the hybrid milieu of the Hamras of Kufa whose Tamimite and 'Abdite Arab *ahlaf* (tribal confederacies) caused them to know and love Salman.

Analysis of the "Prologue"; Autobiographical Hadith
or Account Concerning His Conversion

The "prologue," or *khabar* Salman, is an exceptionally long hadith when compared to analogous accounts attributed to other *sahaba*. It is quite old as well, if one thinks that around 150–175 A.H., it had already been disseminated under seven or eight distinct accounts.

He was of Persian origin, from a notable family, either from among the *asawira* (captives) of Fars or from among the *dahaqin* (landed gentry) of Jayy near Isfahan. He himself was born either in Ramhurmuz (according to 'Awf A'rabi, d. 146) or in Arjan near Kazerun and was raised within Mazdaeism, under the name of Mahbih ibn Budkhashan (according to Ibn Manda) or Ruzbih ibn Marzuban. He became a Christian after a walk, visit or hunt (with a prince) where he had listened with admiration, either to the liturgy in a church, or to the exhortations of a hermit in a cave. Having decided to live as an ascetic Christian (*dayrani*), to abstain from meats cooked by the Mazdaens (or slaughtered after bad treatment) and from wine, Salman left his home and went from town to town to live near the masters of asceticism. These places according to various accounts are either Homs, Jerusalem, or Damascus, Mosul, Nisibis, Amorium, or Antioch, Alexandria. He left the last town upon learning of the imminent coming of a prophet "in the land of Teima." His guides, the nomads, betrayed him and sold him as a slave; whether, first at Wadi'-l-Qura (to a Jew), whether, at Yathrib (the year before or after the first year of the Hegira) to a Jew of the Bani Qurayza ('Uthman ibn al-Ashhal), or to a woman (after this Jew) of the tribe of Juhayna or of Sulaym or of the Ansar (i.e., Khalisa, daughter of a *halif* (ally) of the Bani Najjar) for whom he kept the vineyard. Upon hearing of Muhammad, he went to find him, whether in Mecca, guided by an old woman from Isphahan, or in Quba (near Medina). He recognized in him the three personal signs for which he was seeking: refusal of simony (the diversion to his own personal meal of the offerings given for the benefit of his community = *sadaqa*), the acceptance for his personal meal of strictly private offerings (*hadya*), and the presence of the prophetic seal, a fleshy growth on the right shoulder. This account ends with the (exchange of letters) *mukataba:* Salman is released from bondage for the sum of 360 suckers of transplanted dates and 40 oques of gold. His new co-religionists joined together to pay his ransom (Sa'd ibn 'Ubada would have provided 60 suckers).

In comparing the seven accounts of this prologue, one sees that while generally respecting the frame of the canvas, slight but very skillful retouches, sufficient for changing this and that, were made to certain episodes. The enumeration of the masters of asceticism (changed from three to ten) was conceived as a hierarchic gradation leading Salman into direct contact, either with the *wasi* of Jesus, or with Jesus himself (in a vision in Medina) as a covering of the interval (from "250" to "500" years) that had passed from Jesus to Muhammad, thus making of Salman a contemporary Methuselah. . . .

Once the slave ransom was effected, how was Salman, a non-Arab foreigner, able to be admitted into the young Muslim community of Medina? Ransomed by a collectivity, he must have become the collective freedman of those who were grouped together. However, he is pointed out later as the personal freedman of the Prophet. In order to resolve the difficulty, he was made to participate in Medina in the rite of fraternization (*muwakha*) which before the Battle of Badr linked the *muhajirun* [those on the Hegira with Muhammad], one by one, to their hosts in Medina, the Ansar. . . .

The Hadith "Salmān minna Ahl al Bayt"

The intimacy of Salman with the Prophet and his household, since he began to live with them, outside of little histories of no import, is based on this phrase, "Salman is one of us, we, the people of the House," which Sunni tradition has made to be uttered by Muhammad in the year 5, at the time of the Battle of the Trench. The Prophet would have settled the debate between Muhajir (companions from Mecca) and Ansar (protectors in Medina) concerning Salman, by thus including him among his personal adherents. . . .

Affirming that Salman would have been made part, as a client, of the "people of the Household," it was said that his name could be read among theirs in the register of pensions (*diwan al-'ata*) under Caliph 'Umar; inscribed for 4,000 to 6,000 dirhams – an exceptional figure, since Salman had not been at the Battle of Badr; Horovitz therefore had reason to take exception to this pseudo-proof.

Without adopting Ahmad Aqaeff's hypothesis concerning the secret anti-Sunni society which Salman was supposed to have set up with some Iranian "converts" – it is reasonable to believe that, from the end of the first century, the formula of Salmanian adoption had, among many Shi'ites, a ritual importance, derived from the very inspiration of the Prophet, an importance which it has not ceased to preserve, to this day, closely linking Salman to the Prophet, at the time of the revelation of the Qur'an.

His Death in Mada'in; Evidence Concerning His Arrival in Iraq as Halif of the Abdalqays

Ibn 'Abd al-Barr (d. 463) gives us, based on Sha'bi (d. 103), the following information: "Salman died in Mada'in, in a *'ulayya* (Meccan expression for *ghurfa*, a one-room apartment) belonging to Abu Qurra." This exact detail may be authentic. Abu Qurra Kindi, qadi of Kufa in the year 17 A.H., has left us through his son 'Amr (living in 83 A.H.), a series of facts concerning Salman which constitute the principal Kindi source (before Zadhan), that is said to be from the Al Abi Qurra.

In any case, a "tomb (*qabr*) of Salman" was erected in Mada'in when the first respite from persecutions, from 204–232 A.H., permitted the Shi'ites to raise one to Ali and to Husayn. The Zaidi Ibn Shayba Sadusi (d. 262) has indicated it. In the fourth

century, Muqaddasi mentions it; later al-Khatib; Yaqut went
there on pilgrimage. Up until now, two categories of pilgrims
go there: certain Sunni guilds from Baghdad (barbers, chiropo-
dists, phlebotomists and surgeons' aids) on the traditional anniversary of the fifteenth of Shaban (beginning in the seventh century); and at various dates, individual Shi'ites returning from
Najaf and Karbala. In the seventh century, Mada'in, still a village (*qarya*) of farm laborers, sheltered only ardent Shi'ites
(women could only go out after nightfall). It was the same in
the fourth century, when this place was the center of the extremist Shi'ite sect, the Ishaqiya. Likewise, already in the second century, since Nawbakhti states that "all the people of Mada'in are Shi'ite extremists," with regard to the foundation among
them of the extremist sect of the Harithiya (before 127 A.H.),
which had some *hadith* concerning Salman. Going back still
further, we note that Sabat, on the western outskirts of Mada'in,
was, after 37 A.H., the place of exile and refuge of the extremist
'Abdallah ibn Wahb Hamdani (the famous Ibn Saba). All this
makes one think of the attraction of a pre-existent, venerated
tomb more than of the sudden flowering of an arbitrary locali-
zation at this site.

The other *mashhad* of Salman reported in Dameghan, Quhab
(northeast of Isphahan), Sudud, and Jerusalem, are indeed arbitrary placements and do not appear until the sixth century.

The date of Salman's death is not known—"at the end of the
Caliphate of 'Umar," or "during the Caliphate of 'Uthman"
(Waqidi, Ibn Sa'd)—because apparently "he had moved to Kufa
during the Caliphate of 'Uthman" (Ibn Shayba). In the third
century A.H. the compilers of Sunni hadith fixed the date as
the year 36 A.H. They did so because his presence at the defeat
of Balanjar in 32 A.H. gave a *terminus a quo*. Certain people put
his death earlier in 33 A.H. because Ibn Mas'ud, who died in
34 A.H., was said to have been present together with Sa'd (ibn
Malik = A.S. Khudri) during his death throes.

By referring to the sources, I would be inclined to put his
death in Mada'in between the years 20 and 28 A.H.

The accounts of his death are enigmatic. Salman had a bit of perfume spread about, greeted the *ahl al-qubur*, and demanded to be left alone with all the doors open, as if awaiting invisible visitors. That is where the Sunni versions stop. But the Shi'ite tradition, *ab antiquo*, specified that it was not a question of angels, but rather Ali, the Prophet's son-in-law, who was transported miraculously from Medina to be present at his death. And this legend, which displeased the later 'Abbasid Caliph Mustansir, appears to be very old but was perhaps very early.

What Was Salman to the Prophet?

The Ismaili Shi'ites claimed that it was Salman, in fact, who had made Muhammad retain the entire Qur'an and that the Angel Gabriel was nothing more than the conventional name which this divine mission had granted to Salman. The Ismailis are Muslims who envisage a particular modality of inspiration, wherein the dictation by the invisible angel is replaced by initiation, soul to soul, communicated to the Prophet, by divine command, by his companion. The hadith which they invoke are questionable, and their theory turns up again in later neo-gnostic speculations.

The personal relationships historically possible between Salman and the Prophet are reduced to the following:

(1) According to an anonymous Sunni source from Ibn Ishaq: Salman was one of the sixteen companions who, upon arriving in Medina, were allowed to participate in the rite of fraternization; one of the seventeen *mawla* of the Prophet (but soon freed). This raises the very interesting question of the *sadaqat al Nabi*, of the enclosed gardens (*hitan*) in which the household of the Prophet lived in Medinah, and of the names of the beneficiaries. It is from the *hayit* Maythab that the palm plants came which were to pay (with gold) the ransom of Salman.

Finally, Salman occupies the second rank in the list of the

thirty-four *ahl-al-suffa* compiled in the fourth century by the historian of Sufism, Sulami; but the majority of Sufi authors avoid citing him, although he is one of the principal ascetics among the *sahaba*.

(2) According to the Zaidi Shi'ites, Salman was chosen by the Prophet as one of his twelve or fourteen *nujaba* (noblemen). He was even proclaimed the one of the Four Companions (with Ali, Abu Dharr, and Miqdad) whom God ordered Muhammad to prefer; and the third of the Three Elect "whom Paradise desires" (after Ali and Ammar). These beginnings of veneration represent everything that the bourgeoning Zaidism could accept from a Shi'ite devotion, which must therefore have begun before 113–121 A.H.

(3) According to the moderate Imami Shi'ites, Salman, the first of the Three Apostles (*hawariyun;* with Miqdad and Abu Dharr) of Muhammad, was his confidant, his privileged counselor; his exceptional adoption was designed to exercise the same role after his death, next to his legitimate heir, Ali, to whom the Prophet had made him swear loyalty, with five other companions, in private.

What is the role of Salman after the death of the Prophet? The question scarcely exists for the Zaidis, but for the Imami Shi'ites, on the contrary, the mission of Salman expands. He becomes the privileged counselor allied by the Prophet to Ali, and the one who must teach the Muslims to recognize in the latter the legitimate leader, the Imam, secretly, by initiating believers into the growing Imami sect. He is one of the seven faithful protestors, with whom Ali buried Fatima by night, one of the four *arkan* (upholding leaders) ready to draw the sword and one of the three who in fact effectively drew the sword. He is the first among them in dignity, concludes the Imami dogma. The Imami history thus appears to include an anachronism in representing Salman with weapons in hand.

In reflecting upon the role of Salman, the Imamis take it for granted that the spirit of exegesis (*ta'wil*), which for us "opens the meaning of the Scriptures," is distinct from the spirit (Gabriel) who dictated the text (*tanzil*) to Muhammad; that Salman is superior to him, that he is part of the Qur'anic *Ruh al-amr,* a kind of divine emanation realizing gradually all the secret designs of God. Salman is one of the instruments of this, one of the instrumental causes (*asbab:* cf. Qur'an 22:15, etc.) as much in relation to the Prophet as to Ali. This *Ruh,* executor of divine decisions, explains the permanent norms to those whom it chooses as its instruments.

Thus, Salman acquires, in Shi'ite gnosis, his definitive aspect. He is the indispensable "missing link" between Muhammad and Ali; and all the ingenuity of the extremist theologians was exercised to formulate the reciprocal relations of the three spiritual prototypes corresponding to these three historical personalities: the *'Ayn* (to Ali), the *Mim* (to Muhammad), and the *Sin* (to Salman).

It must be pointed out that, contrary to the accusations of the Sunni heresiographers, never did an extremist Shi'ite sect claim that any of these three archetypes was able to be God through essence. It is a question only of a deification by participation, the mode of participation differing according to the archetype preferred by the sect.

The *'Ayn* is the prototype of the Imam (Adam to Sujud, Ali to Ghadir), with its seat at the center, immobile and silent (*Samit*), mysterious and immanent, like the divine commandment. It presides in permanence over the universe, in a single form, but sometimes fivefold, of a commander of divine law. It is the sign (*ma'na*) which situates God at the center of the community; it veils and reveals an invisible presence. It is the permanent root of the vocation of the Imamate, its divine and immortal seed, soon confused with plastic matter, the hereditary flesh of the race elected to the Imamate (*ahl al-istifa'iya;* Banu'l-Sad). It is the seed which traverses, carried from male to male, the generations. For this tradition, in order to die a good Muslim, it is necessary to recognize this manifestation and to love it in these intermittent appearances, which are periodic as the return of the crescent moon (*'awdat al-'urjun*), and which, alone, regulates canonical acts (*sawm hajj, 'idda, 'ila*).

The *Mim,* prototype of the Nabi (especially of Muhammad),

is mobile and expressive (*natiq*); its public preaching (*da'wa*) victoriously promulgates the divine decisions. It thus designates and names the personification (be it unique or fivefold) of the *'Ayn*. It is the Name (*Ism*) by which the faithful invoke God. Like the formula of science, which evokes the idea for the mind (without intervening in its understanding), the *Mim* is a gate of a wall which it is necessary to go through, because it masks.

The *Sin*, prototype of the *asbab*, consists of supernatural links which can link heaven to earth (cf. Qur'an 27:15), especially through Salman, and is the instrument of initiation. It attracts one to divine counsel through persuasion, just as the call (*nida'*) of the muezzin recalls the prayer in the heart. It is the door (*bab*) which filters the illuminating light (*nur sha'sha'ani*), where the believer joins the Presence. It realizes the divine work, it inhales the Spirit (*Ruh*) engendering the body and initiating souls. It is the power (*qudra*) which gives life (*wujud*).

From there flow three different conceptions of divine action in the Muslim community:

According to the Siniya, it is the penetration (*hulul*) of the *Ruh*, divine emanation inspiring the *Sin* and, through it, illuminating, sanctifying, and elevating gradually up to the luminous "angelic" state, all the faithful souls, even the *'Ayn* and the *Mim*.

According to the 'Ayniya, it is miraculous occultation (*taghyib*) of the person of the Imam, invisibly eliminated (not transfigured) in order to represent (like a phantom) the supreme authority of God, the *'Ayn*. Then the *'Ayn* introduces the creative locution of the *Mim* in the immaterial diction of the *Sin*, which itself breathes its orders into the initiates.

According to the Mimiya, it is the gradual explication, the growth, through its own virtue, of the Enunciator of the Law, the *Mim* (materialization of the *Ruh*), which imprints its commandments upon the pure receptivity of the *'Ayn*, and causes the universe to be organized by subalternate personifications (= the *Sin*).

It is not forbidden to think that the Prophet, along with his great political collaborators, those interested and suspected who

rallied to him, closer to his own heart than the diplomatic in-
triguers of his harem, had trustworthy friends and that next to
and above his wife Khadija and his slave Zaid, came Hudhayfa
and Salman. One can also suppose that next to the energetic
faith of Muhammad in his Abrahamic lineage and in his vocation as warner (*nadhir*), there was the ascetic's passion for justice, anxiously awaiting the victory of a Qayim, of a judge guided
by the Spirit, who would finally extirpate simony and would
penetrate hypocritical hearts.

On one memorable day, Shi'ite tradition tells us, Salman attended the *mubahala* (the trial by fire on the fourth of Shawwal
in the year 10 = January 15, 631 A.D.). In Medina, at the cemetery of al-Baqi' near the "red dune," Muhammad, faced with
Christian envoys from the Belharith of Najran, had assigned
to them a judgment of God (Qur'an 3:54). For this ordeal, the
unique manifestation of his total sincerity, Muhammad constituted as "his own" the "Five whom he covered with his cloak":
his two grandsons, his daughter and son-in-law, as hostages of
his faith in his prophetic mission. From then on, for certain
friends of the Prophet, the affection which they felt for the Five
was transformed and became a devotional love. They venerated
the Alids because their close biological parentage was found
transfigured by a solemn judiciary substitution, transferring to
them all their hope of justice when the Prophet died. Others,
confronted with them, hated them, transferring onto the Alids
their vendetta, the *thar* of their pagan dead killed at Badr, at
the order of Muhammad, by the hand of Ali. With the premature disappearance of the Prophet, this *a'zam musiba* of the old
funerary epitaphs, Salman had to clarify and state his convic-
tions, inaugurating in Iraq among the Abdalqays, the legitimist
movement, well before Abu Dharr and Ammar. Ali became
aware only gradually of the tragic destiny which this judiciary
substitution of the Prophet had reserved for him in the Muslim
community. He took an attitude of commander of divine law,
Nazzam remarks, only when confronted with the Kharijite se-
cessionist rebels, who killed him in the year of the *Mim,* 40 A.H.
Still more consciously, his second son and successor, Husayn,

was to assume all of this destiny, going to be killed "for the sake of justice" in Kerbala in 60 A.H., the year of the *Sin*.

Salman died before them surely but, in Islam, this desire for temporal justice which he had witnessed and which became Shi'ism was to be transformed also into a thirst for eternal life. Shi'ite devotion to the legitimist prophetic cause and to the anticipated Mahdi, and Sufism through its mystical vocations, trace their origins back to Salman. Better than to anyone else the famous words of Imam Ja'far, which later became a Sunni hadith, apply to this foreigner, who came to Islam from so far: *"bada'l-Islam ghariba, fasaya'ud ghariba, kama bada; fatuba li'l-ghuraba min Ummati Muhammad"*: "Islam began in exile (in Medina), and will go again into exile (in Kufa, or in Jerusalem, its first and its last *qibla*), as it began, and happy are those among the members of the Community of Muhammad who will go into exile (in order to find again the Qayim)."

Was Avicenna, the Philosopher, Also a Mystic?

(1954)

The word "mystic" has been so generalized in its diverse usages, especially in our time, that we must recall briefly its basic meaning. It is the experience, unprovoked, of the unexpected, of the inexplicable, of the unique, of the individual, of the instant, that may be of joy or of suffering; an experience that is surely "subjective" but whose subject intends to remain passive, in the embrace of the real, in order to conceive it, in an unpreconceived reception that most psychologists and psychiatrists consider inefficacious and sterile, but which has led many men to "find" their definitive personalities and to share, through an all-powerful compassion, in the suffering and grief of humanity.

Avicenna (in Arabic Ibn Sina) was foremost a philosopher, which, in his time like that of Aristotle, signified first an encyclopaedist knowledgeable in the classification of all sciences, then a comparatist seeking to clarify our knowledges by deducing from them a hierarchical series of principles going back early to the Aristotelian Prime Mover, to a Divinity concerning itself only with general ideas and impersonal souls. Avicenna, born a Muslim, was the son of an Ismaili, that is to say, a gnostic Muslim interposing between him(self) and the jealous God of Abraham (and of the Prophet Muhammad) diverse series of spiritual emanations, of angels "illuminating" human souls imprisoned in the sublunary world.

Avicenna tells us himself that he abandoned the Ismailism

of his father but remained imbued with the syncretist method of the Ikhwan al-Safā', the Ismaili encyclopaedists whose great collective work tried to present in philosophical language, following a very Aristotelian argumentation, a reconciliation between Muslim religion and Hellenistic philosophy. And as the only Muslims daring to examine the philosophical texts translated from Greek were the sect of Avicenna's father, it was among the Ismailis like Nasir i-Khusraw that we see written at that time books entitled *Reconciliation of the Two Wisdoms* (= Greek and Islamic, meaning Ismailism), gnostic syntheses.

Avicenna, more detached from Ismaili practice (apart from his Nayruziya essay on the "symbolic" value of the twenty-eight letters of the Arabic alphabet, which explains the Qur'an by means of barely altered Ismaili initiatory principles), had a choice of two methods of synthesis: gnosticism or mysticism. I mean by "gnosticism" an abstraction from angelology, setting between God and human intelligences abstract principles arbitrarily posed by an implacable religious axiomatic-like basis of a system in the world.

Like Plotinus, Avicenna seems to have opted against the gnostic method for a "mystical" method, for his very Muslim concern (infused with a certain mysticism) with worshipping only One God made him "pare down" the interventions of the Emanations, of the Ten Intelligences, in the ascent of souls toward God. When his indomitable curiosity made him approach the Sufis with this classic problem of the journey of the soul to God, he wrote his *Ishārāt*, the title which I prefer to translate as "Directives" on condition that one senses in this word the "therapeutic directives" of the doctor of the soul, not a technique of mechanical "prescriptions." This book is very unusual, for it uses the experiences of the great early Sufis rather than the personal experience of Avicenna himself (nowhere does he build a "refuge" of recollection, as does Ghazali later), with a serious religious sympathy which will convince the great theologian Fakhr Razi to summarize the *Ishārāt* in order to link mysticism to the body of the new Scholasticism of the Ash'arites. Avicenna had even begun this linkage, witness his usage of the term *'ishq,* desire, used earlier by the Hallajians and, later, in the Basrian school of Abd al-Wahid Ibn Zayd. "Desire," which signified among the Hallajians the very Essence of God, "freely poor with its humblest free creature," is restricted by Avicenna to the meaning of the Necessary Emanation of God, Who causes all creatures to move harmoniously in intertwinings of spherical cycles, in the manner of Plato and the Avicennist Dante.

Mehren has given the name of "mystical treatises" to other writings of Avicenna, which I consider to be much less mystical than the *Ishārāt:* the Epistle of the Birds, Hayy-b-Yaqzan, etc. There are astonishing symbolic accounts of an angelological Gnosis, finalist and eschatological, very different from their Ismaili prototypes, barely "philosophized" but which will become "mystical," and rather disturbingly mystical, only with the retouches which Suhrawardi of Aleppo will bring to them, he the founder of the philosophical school of the Ishraq, which continued the influence of an Avicennism, deepened from the religous point of view, up to our day.

So much for the writings of Avicenna. Now let's turn to his personal life. We lack even the slightest indication of an "interiorization" by him of the public rites of Islam; the commentaries on the Qur'an that Avicenna has left us are purely rationalistic with a gnostic thrust. And as for the "therapeutic directives" of his *Ishārāt,* we have seen that they remained theoretical for him. Indeed, though he was a great physician who cited for us, especially in Persian, many firsthand observations, he did not want to inoculate himself with mysticism in order to understand it, as Ghazali dared to do.

It is good to compare here the temperaments of the two great men. Ghazali will turn to mysticism out of disgust with the uncertainties of all of the sciences that he had passionately studied one after another. He will turn, in a kind of Pascalian wager (he cites this argument moreover in his *Ihyā',* as noted by Asin Palocios) without a spiritual guide, as is his manner, and he will come out of it ending in a kind of marginal philosophy of mysticism.

Avicenna, perhaps out of tact, is hesitant vis-à-vis Transcen-

dence and out of humility as a sinner remains, alas, habitu-
ally in this position until his death. He does not attempt like
Ghazali a vow of poverty, but remains human; and in his correspondence with the Sufi Abu Sa'id Ibn al-Khayr (cited by 'Ayn
al-Qudat Hamadhani, born in his city, both Avicennian and
Ghazalian), he distinguishes clearly between the two domains,
the theoretical (theological) and the practical (mystical). In terms
of his influence on Thomistic theological Scholasticism, Avicenna acts as a monotheist—but from the perspective of
Thomistic theological knowledge, not from the Augustinian
perspective of the savorable wisdom which represents the mystical tradition in Christianity.

If during his lifetime Avicenna approached mysticism with
curiosity and sympathy, after his death the Avicennian school
became divided on the mystical problem as it did on Scholasticism. In the West, the Latin translations of Avicenna contributed to differentiate a Scholasticism that was precisely "laicized,"
desacralized by an Avicennian recourse to Greek philosophy,
from mystical wisdom. (One would have to await the Spanish
mystics, from Lull to St. John of the Cross, to be able to speak
of the influence of Muslim mysticism on Christianity.) In the
East, the Arabic texts of Avicenna served to reduce experiential
mysticism to a sort of consciously monistic Scholasticism. Ibn
Taymiya, a clearsighted adversary, saw him strongly in Ibn
'Arabi, where this "existential" monism is blended through Avicenna in a revitalization of the Ismaili gnosticism of the Ikhwan
al-Safa'. But Ibn Taymiya was mistaken when he traced this existential monism back to the early Sufis who, like Hallaj, wanted
to philosophize mysticism but accepted only testimonial monism
("my witness of the Truth unites me with God"), not existential
monism ("my existence is realized in God"). It is Suhrawardi
who elaborated in his doctrine of *ishraq*, or illumination, a new
Avicennism (the "oriental philosophy" proclaimed by Avicenna
at the end of his life), attempting to reconcile philosophy and
gnosticism (Ismaili tinged with Mazdaism) no longer directly
but by a middle course, an ambiguous mystical element that
is both testimonial and existential. His great Persian disciples

of the seventeenth century derived from this an Imamite philosophy in which Avicenna by his *Ishārāt* is accepted as a mystical doctor, according to the post-mortem interpretation boldly developed by Suhrawardi and the gnostic poems attributed to Avicenna.

Avicenna would hardly recognize himself therein, he whose personal sympathies for mysticism do not seem to have passed the stage, in itself interesting, of a physician who posed a "finalist" diagnosis for curing, or of an aesthetician who, in music, abandons Greek theories to give us the new Persian names of the practical modes used by contemporary musicians to bring about certain states of soul among their listeners.

At the Avicenna conference of April 1954 held in Tehran and Hamadan, the invited Westerners have felt in the communications made at the conference the force of the Muslim affirmation of the divine Transcendence, of the God of Abraham, which releases, without intending to, in the Christian listener a deep impression of mystical desire without images, emptying him of the distressing luxury of sensible imagery with which Christian mysticism is weighted down in our Indo-European languages. Let us affirm that, in the case of Avicenna, Muslim transcendentalism is at its minimum. But it exists, and the Christian is struck by it.

Muslim and Christian Mysticism
in the Middle Ages
(1957)

This problem of cultural comparatism was posed for the first time in a precise way by D. Miguel Asin Palacios, the genial author of the thesis on the Muslim origins of the thematic framework of the *Divine Comedy,* a thesis for which Enrico Cerulli brought forth corroborative documentation very worthy of attention, in *Il Libro della Scala e la questione della fonti arabo-spagnole della Divina Commedia,* which the Vatican published in 1949.

The present communication does not intend to study in detail the incidence of Dantean researches of D. Miguel Asin Palacios on the literature of courtly love, even when they touch closely on mystical literature, as is the case about which I have reflected a great deal of Ibn 'Arabi in his *Tarjumān al-ashwāq* and the *Dhakhayr* on the ideal love of the beautiful Nizam bint Rustum Isfahaniyya, whom he met on pilgrimage to Mecca and sought after later behind the latticework of her *Dar al-Falak* convent in Baghdad. The audience will find similarities here with the *Vita Nuova* and *Il Convito* inspired in Dante by Beatrice. As regards matters of "framework" and stylization of similar subjects, Father Gabrieli is the one who will show you what to think of the comparison of Ibn 'Arabi with Dante. And I shall concentrate as regards this borderline case of ideal Platonic love only on the role of the sister-soul, of the "chosen sister," and of the "companion from on high" in the journey of the Muslim soul to God through its stages. More than any other, Muslim mysticism is the mysticism of transcendence and moves to "God alone, God, the first served."

D. Miguel Asin Palacios, who has grasped this well, has not hesitated to present directly the comparison between the very structure of Muslim mysticism and that of Christian mysticism in the Middle Ages with regard to two cases: the philosophical schematization of mysticism conceived as interreligious, notably in the theological meditation on the *Names of God* in Ibn 'Arabi and Ramon Lull; and in the method of psychological introspection of the *via negativa* in Ibn 'Abbad of Runda and in St. John of the Cross.

In the first case he thought he had definitely resolved the difficulty in enumerating theoretical similarities of technical terminology which appear in Ibn 'Arabi and Ramon Lull on the ground of an interreligious apologetic. In the second case he underlined some practical apothegmatic similarities which Ibn 'Abbad and St. John of the Cross combine for certain sequences of maxims concerning the spiritual direction of consciences.

In both cases, D. Miguel Asin Palacios extended to the domain of comparative mysticism the main hypotheses which had guided him to track down the "Muslim source" of the *Divine Comedy*. And after I criticized his main hypotheses in a long article entitled "Dante et l'Islam," which appeared in *La Revue du Monde Musulman* (Paris 1919, vol. 36, pp. 23–58), my very dear friend responded point by point in a long letter dated February 14, 1920. He asked me at the time not to publish the letter, because he did not want me to cast a slur on our profound friendship by accompanying it with a critical annotation. This letter remains, after more than thirty years, very suggestive; it seems to me today more convincing than it did then, especially in its mystical implications, and this is why I enter it in the proceedings of the debate engaged in here as the first *dialogued* document to be examined.

I had begun the dialogue on three points:

(1) The *beyond the grave* themes, identified by Asin in medieval Christian legends. I objected that, apart from some specific borrowings, I saw only architectonic similarities explainable by the restricted number of alternatives available to the

imagination of the writer; the fact of what we call, since Jung, the archetypes of folklore, proving that it is not a question of real borrowings but of signs of an analogical mental activity provided with the same experimental materials, perhaps authentically theopathic and directed toward the same plan, the same eschatological desire, also perhaps authentic. There is one topic of imagination, indeed among all mystics in both Christianity and Islam, and it is not unthinkable/unlikely that the structure of this topic derives from an *experiential source from above,* which the American school of psychology calls the telepathic coincidences organically derived from converging psychological developments, "constellations" of the profound unconscious. The question of the supernatural character of this "beyond" will not be posed here.

(2) The analogies of the "dolce stil novo," between Dante and Islam.

(3) The laws of literary imitation, applied to comparative mysticism.

Number 2, referring back to that part of the presentation which belongs to the domain of our colleague Father Gabrieli, and number 3 having been repeated and deepened in an analytical way in Chapter II of my *Essai sur les origines du lexique technique de la mystique musulman* (two editions: Paris, 1922 and 1954), I restrict myself to giving here the responses that Asin made to my objections vis-à-vis number 1.

A. The double paradisiacal recompense and the double infernal punishment (*jaza, ihsan; janna, Hadra; a'mal, istifaya*)

Asin responds: "the intellectual parallel between East and West could explain the *dogma* . . . common to Islam and Christianity, but not the *philosophical theory* used to explain it, and even less the artistic painting in Dante and Ibn 'Arabi; because these two factual aspects have no precedents in Christian theology and literature.

I had retorted at the time that the vision of "the meal of Paradise," seen by the brother of St. Perpetua in Carthage, was earlier than Islam; and that the famous Catalonian renegade Ibn al-Tarjuman (Anselm Turmeda) regarded as "specifically Christian" certain visions of "castles of Paradise" still current in Islam.

B. Architectural similarities, the same choice of a guide. . . .

Asin responds: "the coincidences could be explained by a symmetry, if they were reduced to general characteristics, but not when they are extended also to *particular* and *vivid details* which cannot depend on the same manner of reasoning (cf. *Escatologia*, p. 298). *A priori* parallelism is not sufficient to gauge details that are *very numerous* and *very analogous*. If we deny this criterion, all scientific work in the history of ideas would be as useless and false as in the history of the arts. The evolution of *styles* can be explained scientifically only according to this law."

I would answer him now, following my studies on Sura 18 of the Qur'an ("Les VII Dormants, apocalypse de l'Islam," in *Analecta Bollandiana*, Brussels, 1950, vol. 68 [*Mel. P. Peeters*, vol. 2], pp. 245–260) and the role of Khadir-Eliyas, that the guide of Musa (Khadir-Eliyas) and the guide of the Prophet (Gabriel) come from a *higher* world. Just as Beatrice, coming from a higher world, will succeed Virgil to guide Dante to Paradise. The Muslim notion of the "spiritual guide" is, from the beginning, more explicit and more decisive than the Christian notion.

C. The problem of limbo (*al-A'raf*)

I had conceded to Asin that the Latin word *limbus* could translate in the Middle Ages the Arabic word *al-A'raf*. But I had denied, and continue to deny, that the early Qur'anic meaning of *al-A'raf* could be that which the Dantean eschatology (and Christian eschatology in general) gives to the word *limbus*.

The Qur'an's verses 44–45 of Sura 7 are precise: they depict the "people of al-A'raf" ("the Heights") as exceptional human beings, endowed by God with a mystical gift of discernment. Perched on an elevated place that is commanding simultaneously of Paradise and Hell, they express their desire (for the one) and their horror (of the other), and announce, both to the elect and to the damned, the very judgment of God. They are therefore the assistants of the Judge of the Last Judgment, associated with this supreme magistrate *because they have abandoned all to God* (cf. Matt. 12:27), which is the attribute of mystics. Might it be a question of the martyrs and Sufi saints (Hasan Basri, Tustari, Qushayri) or of the twelve martyred Imams of the Shi'ites (*Mufīd, sharh 'aqā'id Saduq*, pp. 196–198 of the Tabriz edition, appended in its *Awā'il*).

Even if later the Mu'tazilite and Hellenistic influence, which such neo-Ash'arites as Ghazali underwent, ascribed to Islam the idea of an *A'raf* peopled with neutered and imperfect beings in a state of suspension, one cannot see how this later Muslim idea could have influenced the Christian *limbo,* which was reserved for children who died unbaptized or for adults deprived of discernment.

Asin again responded prudently: "I said nothing of the Qur'anic meaning *in se,* but *in quantum* it has been interpreted by the hadith. And the hadith that I cited are neither 'rather modern' nor dependent on Ghazali" (cf. *Escatologia,* p. 186, nn.2 and 3).

D. The solemn intercession of the Virgin Mary at the Last Judgment

Emile Mâle, astonished by the rapid growth of this Marian doctrine in the thirteenth century, had claimed to have seen a Franciscan innovation behind it. Asin, sharing his astonishment, prefers to see it, shall we say, as a Christian imitation of the *Shafa'a,* of the intercession of the Prophet Muhammad, verified by the ancient popular devotion of the *tasliya* that "God bestows upon the Prophet and his family," as He bestowed upon Abraham and his.

Asin responded: "What I said (*Escatologia,* pp. 254–255) has no connection with the cult of the holy virgin, but only with the intervention of Mary and St. John on the Day of Judgment. This belief is contrary to the dogma as it is interpreted in the *Dies irae* and elsewhere."

I had responded to him, in 1919, that the rise of the Marian intercession (dogma) was witnessed in the East before Islam, at the time of the *theotokos* definition of 431 in Ephesus. Now, after my researches (*Les fouilles archéologiques d'Ephèse,* in *Mardis de Dār es Salam,* Cairo, 1952) into the very unusual parallel between the development of the Islamic *Shafa'a* and the rise of the Marian *hyperdulia* in the Christian church, I am forced to state that there is not only a parallel but indeed a "mental" convergence. In other words, I believe that, since the end of its evolutionary process has led it to its primordial origin, the Muhammadian *Shafa'a* goes back more and more to the pre-existence of the *Fitra,* of the *Nur Muhammadi,* like the Marian hyperdulia to the Immaculate Conception, and that these two ideas are at bottom identical.

This convergence is confirmed by the rise of similar devotions such as the rosary (*tasbih*) and the scapulary (*khirqa*). Asin answered me: "Your remark about the rosary and the scapulary touches on two interesting problems," and he concluded with the borrowing by Islam of the scapulary and by Christianity of the rosary. I saw in this rather two convergent psychological developments, focussed on two profound "constellations" of the unconscious. My study of "l'hyperdulia de Fatima" in relation to the Marian hyperdulia includes some very significant Ismaili texts.

One sees that when detailed similarities are pointed out between the two forms, Muslim and Christian, of a theme of religious meditation, Asin does his utmost to remain on the literal ground of borrowings. He wrote me again, and this brought forth the mystical comparison between the *Vita Nuova* and the *Tarjumān al-Ashwāq:* ". . . I do not believe that in order to imitate *freely* and with intentions *different* from those of his models, Dante needed to make himself a Muslim by desire. Note how many Christian thinkers, writers of romances, and poets of the Middle Ages imitated Arabic models without thinking at all of sharing in the concrete intentions for which these models had been created. Man, and even more the artist, is a machine who is less ingenuous, less sincere, and less spontaneous than you think him to be. He profits from everything which seems to him good to imitate in his work, without concerning himself with caring about the intention of the author of his model. Note for example the Turmeda case (Abdallah al-Turjuman): this is a Christian priest who became a very zealous and fierce Muslim. And yet Turmeda imitates the Ikhwan al-Safa' in order to compose a book whose central idea is to prove that man is superior to the animals, *because God is incarnated in man.* [N.B.: Ismaili incarnation is not Christian—L.M.]

"Where is the basic parallel of intention here? You say: it is a plagiarism [N.B.: no—L.M.]. How much is the psychology of writers a labyrinth? Dante was not a Turmeda, just as he was not a Lull. . . .

"You believe too much in spontaneous invention. [L.M.: I reacted against the bookish illusion of scribes, which believes that any work of thought arises from an unconscious combining of texts by memory. The experimental science of man is not reduced to this single motive.] The phrase *perinde ac cadaver* seems to you a reinvention of St. Francis and St. Ignatius, wholly symmetrical to that of Tustari. There is no question of invention in either of the two cases; we are dealing with a simple imitation of the monastic literature of the East made independently by Muslims and by monks of the Christian West. [L.M.: I persist in thinking that it is because both of them were bound to analogous disciplines of the ascetical life that they were led to choose the same image and to insist on it as a *rule of action.* It is within these same limits that one loves the same, that one thinks the same, and that one expresses oneself the same. In a hermitage in which one dies without gravediggers, the image, the 'perinde ac cadaver,' is an immediate mental shock.] St. Nilas and St. John Climacus in the East used it (i.e., this approach) before Islam; Tustari, just like Ibn 'Arabi, repeated it. And on the other side, St. Benedict, St. Columban, and St. Fructueux (*sic*) also used it before St. Francis and St. Ignatius. See my 'Bosque jo de un diccionario tecnico de filosofía y teologia musulmana,' in *Rev. de Aragón,* Zaragoza, 1903, pp. 37–39, in which I developed some themes of parallel imitations of an actual Christian model for some other aspects of monastic life; for example, for the personal examination of conscience, conducted with the aid of a little manual, among Christians and Muslims. . . ."

This discussion with Asin permits us to set forth a minimum outline of dogmatic ideas, of practical religion, in which the meditation of mysticism is concentrated. Asin thinks that, in order to deal scientifically with the psychological problem of mysticism, it suffices, as in every other "science," to present a basic axiom, a bundle of arbitrary definitions, from which reason then draws a collection of correct deductions [according to the original axiom]; these are used finally to *explain* the collection of recorded phenomena in the books of the mystics.

He had not yet studied closely the *Munqidh* of Ghazali, in which this great spirit, driven by the layman's intense passion to understand, avows that the study of mysticism is not like the study of other disciplines such as law, philosophy, and theology, in which it is sufficient to absorb through hypothesis the fundamental axioms in order to reconstruct and even extend the rational deductions implied in their premises. To understand mysticism one must have experienced, and willingly, the trials and sufferings of the most humble life. Junayd had said forcefully "we have not learned this science (of mysticism) by means of 'it is said' (*qil waqal*), but by privations and separations from dear ones": applied asceticism.

It is this initiation in "mental scouring" which is the axiom, not theoretical but practical, of mysticism. In our [aforementioned] *Essai* we have shown that the basic technical terms of Muslim mysticism, those inducing words of so many vocations of the perfect life, were "discovered" experientially by the great early Muslim mystics of the first three centuries of the Hegira: as "remarkable points" along the personal life curve of each, as stages, *manazil, maqamat.* These terms, which intoxicate the profane with a beauty that is more than literary, are only promptings, or rather *break-throughs,* which show them how to resolve the general problem of mysticism (within the limits of their capacity of) "feeling" by "vital" interiorization of the personal explanation that they seek to know. These terms are common words, but ones which have undergone an original "minting," which the Muslim canonists call the *majaz shar'i,* the "statutory figurative meaning" for the Qur'anic law, and that we might call here the *majaz ilhami,* the "spiritually figurative meaning" or, in a word, the *"anagogical* meaning."

Whether *shar'i* or *ilhami,* the Muslim technical term is Arabic in origin; it was "found" only by the personal meditation on significant forms of the Arabic language, which is characteristic of all authentic *Semitic* cultural evolution. I return to my study entitled "La structure primitive de l'analyse grammaticale en arabe" (*Arabica* I, pp. 3–16), which deals with the symbolic circle called *dustur al-kitaba* of the "etymological" triliteralism of roots, of the flexional triplicity of the *I'rab,* or of the semantic involution (*tadmin*) of the concept. The vocabulary of Muslim mysticism is not a patchwork of isolated borrowing, lifted from Greek neo-Platonism or from a hypothetical Indo-Iranian tradition; it is the fruit of a "constellation" of convergent mental experiences, lived in Arabic, the liturgical language of prayer.

Are we dealing here merely, as in the case of the archetypes of international folklore, with coincidences drawn from a commonplace topic of the human imagination, compelling our feet to stand in the prints of our predecessors, as Ghazali said, or is it a question of efficacious intersigns, of "theopathic locutions," causing the main intentions of our lives to converge according to the finality even of a divine grace? The problem can only be posed. Mystical life is above all an anagogical interpretation of our *weltanschauung,* in which we become aware of the unity of the universe through the prism of the data of Holy Scripture: the Bible for Jews, the Bible together with the Gospels for Christians, the Qur'an, which is a summary of the Bible and the Gospels, for Muslims. Thus giving a real and personal, "inducing" meaning to social roles and to maxims of behavior which are found mentioned therein.

The mystical life would be completely anarchistic and would rebel against the canonical law if it did not find among the legendary roles of scriptural personages a *spiritual guidance* and among their maxims of behavior a *rule of life.*

The messianic idea permitted Christians to choose, beginning with Abraham, a series of historic figures specifying gradually the main features of that union with God realized by the Messiah of Israel under the "theandric" form for Christianity. The call of God has been for all a "call to the desert," since Abraham left the townsman's life for the life of pastoral wandering, Elias and the paneremos of the Essenes along the Dead Sea, up to the Ephesus of the three privileged witnesses of Calvary, up to the Egypt of the desert fathers, and up to the spiritual desert of the Benedictines of every observance. (Note: *Les VII Dormants d'Ephèse* by L.M., Emile Dermenghem, Lounis Mahfoud, Suhayl Unver, and Nicholas de Witt, in *Revue des Études Islamique* [Paris, 1954], pp. 59–112, with 15 plates.)

In Islam, apart from the isolated verses, the Qur'an contains one exceptional sura, the eighteenth, *Ahl al-kahf,* "the Seven Sleepers [of the Cave]," which permitted Muslim religious to profess that there was only one *rule of life,* that of the Seven Sleepers of Ephesus, those Christian martyrs buried alive in the Cave of Perfect Abandonment where the love of Christ attained its plenitude after 309 years, glorified and justified them by an awaited quasi-resurrection, for by being buried alive these (martyrs) practiced to an absolute degree the poverty which is one with the purity of perpetual fasting and obedience.

This Sura 18 also teaches that there is only one spiritual guide reviving over the centuries for the saints the rule of perfection; this is the anonymous sage who dialogued with Moses (as at Tabor, later), the one whom Muslim tradition calls Khadir-Elias, the Elias of Carmel (see L.M., *Elie et son rôle transhistorique, "Khadiriya" in Islam,* in *Études Carmélitaines,* 1955, vol. 2). This is the sage who practices the works of mercy which surpass all others, which give the spirit of consolation and of life.

One should note the elliptical force of mystical meditation in Islam. In Islam where God is inaccessible this meditation wishes to attain by the strictest simplicity a single rule, a single vow, a single guide, a single work of mercy, and in Christianity

—for all the expansion of rules, of vows, of guides and inter-
cessors, and works of zeal—this is what it all comes down to
in the end.

I return to Chapter IV of my *Essai* for the critique of the
famous hadith "la rahbaniyyata fi'l-Islam," "no monkery in
Islam."

For the psychology of the founder of Islam I should say briefly
that, without insisting as much as does Ghazali on the "amor-
ous" fervor of his solitary recollection on Mt. Hira, it is difficult
to deny the "militant" mystical tendency of the prayer of this
orphan: "No one will arbitrate for me with God" (Qur'an 78:22);
his audacious attempt to intercede for his community of faithful by restoring the liturgy of the sacrifice of Abraham; his nocturnal ecstasy toward Jerusalem (and the *mihrab* of Zachariah;
his first *qibla*); his veneration for the *shahada* ("no divinity except God"), in this stoical world of reasoning and argument in
which the negative universal is empirical, not ontological, and
can be transcended by the positively affirmative preposition "except God": this God who is not the law of laws, the Greek demi-
urge, but the Miracle of miracles, the God of Abraham, of Isaac
and of Jacob, as Pascal said.

If the Qur'an, then the Sunna with the Hadith Qudsi (which
represent in fact the first "theopathic locutions" felt in their
hearts by the earliest Muslim mystics, from Hasan Basri to Ibra-
him ibn Edhem and 'Abd al-Wahid ibn Zayd), are the fundamental sources of the Muslim mystical lexicon, this purely
Semitic lexicon of private supererogatory prayer underwent the
"test" of foreign cultures: through Syriac, the Hellenistic philosophical culture of the Christian ascetical school (Wensinck
studied them apropos of Isaac of Nineveh), and the terminology of Hindu-Iranians (atheist Buddhism). But it is useless to
look in these foreign cultures for the origin of Muslim mysticism. As patently useless as is searching for the sources of Christian mysticism (which came from the Essenes) in the hermetic,
Orphic, or Avestan texts.

We maintain that language is essential to the expression of
all authentic mysticism, that language gives to thought its "mor-

dent," that it is the militant act par excellence, the sword that no sin's filth sullies when it pierces through to witnessing the truth.

The "science of hearts" (*'ilm al-qulub*), the early nucleus of the methodological traits of mysticism in Islam, began with the identifying of anomalies in the spiritual life of the believer who prays, who must be simple and naked; the early technical terms served to designate the errors of judgment, the mental pretences, the hypocrisies, all of which the literalist believes characterize collectively as *waswasa* or the incitements of Satan.

The "heart" designates the incessant oscillation of the human will which beats like the pulse under the impulse of various passions, an impulse which must be stabilized by the Essential Desire, one single God. Introspection must guide us to tear through the concentric "veils" which ensheathe the heart, and hide from us the virginal point, the secret (*sirr*) wherein God manifests Himself. Following Hasan Basri, Muhasibi, "the one who submits his conscience to scrutiny," constructed a very beautiful manual of introspection, the *Ri'āya*, edited by Margaret Smith in 1940: it begins with a profound study of the Gospel parable of the sower, though the source is not given.

A contemporary of Muhasibi, the Eygptian Dhu'l-Nun Misri, moved from a study of the deficiencies of our inner life, from a negative critique, to the positive study of the stages of perfection accessible to the soul of the ascetic, stages (ascended by personal effort: *maqamat*) or states (dispensed by grace: *ahwal*): stages that Union enables us to exceed.

Muhasibi may be more important for his other book, the *Nasā'ih*, in which he shows that the guiding principle of mystical unification for his spiritual life was his compassion for the dissension which tore apart the community of Islam; dissension that he had surmounted by attaching himself to a chain of pure witnesses who suffered for the justice of God: making Him loved by other sufferers among the faithful. That is like a sketch of the famous autobiography of Ghazali, the *Munqidh*. The *Munqidh* has been compared to the *Confessions* of St. Augustine, but the latter presents his spiritual itinerary chronologically, whereas Ghazali forms his according to a philosophical classification of disciplines of thought with brief personal remarks.

Then come two impassioned witnesses of the divine personal Unity: Bistami and Hallaj.

Bistami, who used Arabic liturgical terms overlaid with ejaculatory prayers in dialectual Persian (most of which has been transmitted to us only in Arabic transposition), seems to have been endowed with an extraordinary ascetical will, and his flashing words sparkle in quasi-theopathic locutions that are unfortunately uncontrollable, given the wild nature of the subject and the rough condition of the transmission of the texts.

Hallaj, though also born in Persia, had forgotten the Persian of his childhood and had studied thoroughly both Arabic and Islam. Moreover he shared with Eckhart the very rare gift of being able to analyze ecstatic states even while participating in them. We have a sufficient number of authentic texts by him to evaluate his mysticism that he preached publicly and that led him to a long trial followed by a cruel punishment. He lived his prayer, making of the *bismillah* ("in the name of God . . .") the *kun* (the *fiat*). He offered his life, turned toward the *qibla* of Mecca, like the symbolic victims of the Pilgrimage, for the annual pardon of the Islamic community.

"The momentary witness, in the present, of the Witness of Eternity (= the Spirit)," he took part in a chain of apotropaic witnesses of the Truth; he died by the Law and for the Law which condemned him—like Joan of Arc.

After Hallaj we can move on to the one whom since Qutb Qastallani (see *Mélanges Joseph Maréchal,* Brussels-Paris, 1950 vol. 2, p. 292; Sakhawi, ms. Berl. 2849, 7 43[b] [according to Abu Hayan Jayyani, *Kitāb al-nidār*]) the jurisconsults regard as having given the correct formula for the mystical realization consummated in Hallaj: Ibn 'Arabi.

The danger in the Hallajian position was the personal divinization of the witness, the martyr, with a dualistic nuance of Satanism. This Ibn 'Arabi, endowed with an exceptional philosophical temperament, rather more Ismailian than directly Hellenistic in nature, did his utmost to avoid. By means of a complex theory of cyclical emanation coming from and returning to God, and manifesting in God His existence in order to immerse Himself after having passed through the "five worlds" in His unknowable, impersonal, and silent Essence. In this there is no longer concern with preaching, with contending in the community, but with reaching a quietistic serenity in which there is no longer a "you" or a "me" or a "we," nor even a "He."

Parallel to the teaching of Ibn 'Arabi, which in fact deprived the Muslim social evolution of an indispensable intellectual elite, the people attempted to stir group "revivals" through sessions of *dhikr*, litanies chanted and intoned which were aimed at arousing ecstacy. To remember God together is clearly more "real" than to think of God in silence, immobile, alone. But it is strange that in Islam, for which the temporal and the spiritual are indivisible, the influence of Ibn 'Arabi had ended up (or, led to) depriving the Muslim community of the participation of mystics in the works of charity and mercy which give to any human group its fraternal cohesion. It is only in the last hundred years, under the influence of the Christian colonial invasion, that certain Muslim congregations have restored a sense of social mutual-aid: in the beginning in the form of defense of the *mustad'afin* (the oppressed), meaning the holy war against the capitalist and banking infiltration from Europe and America, the silent mobilization of the Muslim faithful in the name of the divine transcendence that every temporal power must recognize against the fetishism of Mammon.

The rapid reconsideration of the leading figures of medieval Muslim mysticism ends in the thirteenth century, from the external point of view of terminology, in what Asin called "el Islam cristianizado"; apropos of Ibn 'Arabi, who died in 1240 of our era.

If one approaches this on the physical plane of the "influences, exchanges, and borrowings," the first six centuries of Islam end:

(1) in a structural influence of the Scholastic presentation of Muslim theology on the formation of Latin Catholic Scholasticism, both Scotist and Thomist. This Asin has underlined, significantly, as "el *averroismo* teologico de S. Tomas de Aquinas." It is a genuine influence, moreover, of a monotheism rigorously transcendent of Sura *al-Ikhlās* (Qur'an 112), which is found exactly formulated in a canon of the Lateran Council of 1209 on the Divine Essence;

(2) in an influence of an inverse sense of the philosophical presentation of a Christianized neo-Platonic mysticism on the doctrine of existential monism (*wahdat al-wujud*), elaborated by Ibn 'Arabi for Islam. Ibn Taymiya called it the Avicennism of the Sufi theoreticians, tracing it back wrongly to Hallaj, in whom, as I have shown in detail in the *Mélanges Joseph Maréchal*, the term *'ishq dhati* ("Essential Desire") does not have the emanationist meaning that it has in Avicennism, but refers to a testimonial monism (*wahdat al-shuhud*) — identical to the conception of the Word among medieval Christian mystics whom the Hellenistic vocabulary had not contaminated. (Note the verse of Hallaj, in *Dīwān* [Paris, 1955], p. 104: "between me and You, there is a 'it is I' which torments me, ah! remove by Your 'it is I,' my 'it is I' from between us.")

This "conception of the Word" is rightfully established in Christianity in a *Marian* form drawn from meditation on the Annunciation and the Visitation, "asymptotic" with the mystery of the Incarnation.

The testimonial monism of Islam, while refusing to accept the possibility of the Incarnation, refers nevertheless, it too, to the Virgin Mary, to the one present *at* the Annunciation; to the one of the Presentation in the Temple (at the *mihrab* of Zachariah, the only sanctuary of the Temple of Jerusalem that the Qur'an mentions), and earlier still to the Immaculate Conception. To the Virgin of Transcendence. To the *Fitra*, to that sign of predestination of the elect that Qarmathian theosophy calls in Arabic "*kuni*" (the feminine form of the imperative *kun*, fiat); whom it venerates undoubtedly as the First Emanation. And whom, through a gnostic tendency, the pantheism of Muslim mysticism stylized by Ibn 'Arabi presents as the ultimate goal of the mystic's ascent, the rediscovery of this ideal essence that the divine thought assigned to it before He created it.

Had there been historically an encounter between these two ideal and *Marian* forms of mysticism: between the Christian and the Muslim forms? Yes, at the end of the Crusades, in September of 1219, at Damietta, when St. Francis of Assisi went to meet the sovereign of Egypt, Malik Kamil, and offered to undergo the ordeal by fire in order to reveal the reality of the Incarnation. We know from St. Bonaventure of the importance of this step in the mystical life of St. Francis. It is this which brought him death from love in his stigmata on Mt. Alvernia, on the day of the Exaltation of the Holy Cross. We know also that this is the summit of Islam which was meant to declare to all humanity that God is inaccessible.

Recent researches have led me to establish further the psychological atmosphere of the appearance of St. Francis before the Sultan at Damietta. I have discovered a Muslim Arabic source which attests that it did indeed take place. Having found in Brusa, thanks to H. Ritter, an unedited work of a Muslim mystic who was an ardent disciple of Hallaj, namely Fakhr al-Din Farisi, I collected documents about his biography. I was able to visit his tomb, in the Qarafa of Cairo, at the feet of the old Egyptian mystic Dhu'l-Nun Misri (whom Egyptian legend, not without anachronism, shows as coming like a bird to bite at the Red Rose that was Hallaj in agony on the gibbet) (in Yūsuf Ahmad, *Turbat al-Fakhr al-Fārisī* [Cairo, 1340 AH], pp. 17–18). And I found in the *Kawākib sayyāra* of Ibn al-Zayyat, edited by Taymur Pasha, that being the spiritual director of Malik Kamil, he had, along with the *rahib* (= Christian monk), a *"hikaya mashhura,"* a celebrated adventure. It does not say that the *rahib* was called Francis, nor that the place was Damietta; further, one can object that Fakhr Farisi, being at the time almost ninety years old (he died six years later), the Sultan would not have taken him to Damietta. But, some years earlier, F. Farisi had made a voyage in Upper Egypt (to Qus), and the Sultan had him brought from Cairo in his entourage on a litter. Finally, two Christian accounts mention the presence close to the Sultan of a religious advisor, an old respected man, "quemdam de presbyteribus suis, virum authenticum et longaevum," "vecchio e reputato sancto" (Golubovish, *BBB, TS,* I, 34, 79), and I think only Fakhr Farisi could have been so identified.

The Christian accounts, which are hostile and ironic, depict this old man leaving the hall hurriedly when he had heard St. Francis propose the trial by fire to the Sultan, not at all intending to participate in it. Was this out of cowardice? The trial by fire was accepted in Islamic law, especially in the thirteenth century, and precisely to cut short the charismatic claims of the mystics. Ibn Taymiya proposed it for the Rafa'iya in Damascus, and Biqa'i cites another case at Rodah in 697/1297 (*Tanbīh,* 149–150). This ordeal is both a Semitic and an ancient Arab tradition, and an application of the Qur'anic principle of the *tahaddi;* the holy war is another such application.

As for the audacious proposal of St. Francis, it is in the medieval chivalric tradition, but it is rash, from the Christian point of view. It is forbidden to tempt God, and Christ did not wish to conquer by ordeal but to suffer a resurgent defeat. It seems that, like the Crusade, which is a calculated counter to the Muslim *jihad* (a Latin counter that the Greek church never accepted), St. Francis became obdurate before the Muslim intransigence at Damietta (like Foucauld, at the end, in the Sahara). And, inversely, mystical Islam softened through submission to the will of God and refused the ordeal as a means to prove its intimate union with God: from Hallaj (in whose case it was an enemy who made him say *"ubahilukum,"* and for whom the legendary trial of the "boiling pot" came long before his execution) up to Fakhr Farisi, who felt that God could perfectly demand that he accept being overcome in the ordeal without any imposture being proven by it. St. Francis, furthermore, on his own, envisioned this eventual abandonment of God during the ordeal, thus pointing out to the Sultan that the trial would prove he was a sinner, not an imposter.

Well before the encounter in Damietta, the Muslim ideal of mystical union collided with the Christian ideal of the Incarnation: during the lifetime of the Prophet, in Medina, a few months before his death, when he received a delegation of Christians from Nejran. In the famous scene of the *mubahala* [in L.M.'s monograph on the subject, Paris 1943 and 1955], the Prophet, to justify God and His holy inaccessibility against the Christian theory of the Incarnation and the divine motherhood of Mary, proposed as an undeniable sign of sincerity recourse to the ordeal in order to settle the matter. Faithful to the Christian idea that one must not tempt God and that the "Cross cannot be conquered because it is defeat itself" (Chesterton), the Christians refused and signed a diplomatic compromise, *musalaha:* the first of the "capitulations."

In a formalist sense, the *mubahala* confronts the two mysticisms: the Islamic and the Christian. Far from opposing them, it makes them converge: for the entire "compassionate" meditation of Muslim souls issues from the participation of a woman, the daughter of the Prophet, *Fatima Umm Abiha,* at the *mubahala,* as the principal hostage of the word of her father; and this made her become in Fatimid meditation the substitute for Mary with respect to the *dhat al-ahzan* and as Virgin of Transcendence with respect to the vow of virginal abandonment to God alone, at the *mihrab* of Zachariah. "Our hearts are one single Virgin, which the dream of no dreamer can penetrate . . . which only the presence of the Lord penetrates in order to be conceived therein" (Hallaj) (*Eranos-Jahrbuch* [Zurich, 1955] 24, pp. 119–132).

The Art of Egypt and the Art of Iraq
(1958)

The economic and social renascence of the Arab world can't fail to have its repercussions on the arts; and it is not unlikely that the artistic rebirth of the Muslim East will be polarized on two axes determined by geography and history, those of Mesopotamia and Egypt.

Egypt, whose double Nile flows along toward the Mediterranean north, toward the olive groves of Syria and Greece from south to north, contrasts with Mesopotamia, whose two rivers bend toward the southeast, toward the Arab date palms of the Persian Gulf, toward the tides and monsoons of the Indian Ocean, toward India and the wide expanse of the southern hemisphere.

If there were only physical conditions identifiable as determining an artistic evolution, Egyptian art could be said to follow the light and airy seraphims, which belong to Egypt, toward an art of Northern lights, of quiet chiaroscuro, whereas Iraqi art would follow the heavy and mighty cherubims, which belong to Mesopotamia, toward an art aglow with tropical splendor.

But the three Abrahamic revelations have come marking the countries of the East with an ideal of abstract transcendence, one without idols, in which forms must give only a brief hint of the Ineffable Name. It is therefore not only the young Egyptian school, but also the young Iraqi school, which must elevate above the massive Assyrian idols the slender silhouette of its symbols, to trace to infinity the circuitous trail of its arabesques. And, in the case of painting, to sublimate the very thick and harsh color pigments to the light colors, to the most diaphanous

134

nuances; as the clash of blues in the Iraqi earthenware triumphs in a celestial blue, *asmanguni*, the old Baghdad treatise from the time of Ma'mun [early 800s A.D.] entitled *Sirr al-khalīqa* ["The Secret of Creation"] shows.

And this is why the name chosen for the new review, *Ishtar*, (and I think also of Esther, of Ecbatana) evokes for this sublimation of epidermal coloration the sunlit bodies which "strip themselves bare" of several myths for the ritual *ihram*, exteriorizing gradually the interior flame, the life of blood in living beings. First, of course, the myth of the seven veils drawn away from the goddess Ishtar during her descent into Hell; the fall of the rebellious archangel in the legend of Salman, who snatches one by one the seven colors of which the veils of the seven heavens are made: according to the *Umm al-Kitāb*.

Muslim legends, by an inverse movement of spiritual abstraction toward the Pure Transcendence, orient artistic abstraction toward the stellar vault, where no longer do only virtual lines draw and individualize, geometrically, the constellations. One might also consider the colored vision of the mystics which lose one by one the "seven primary colors" of their soul in order to annihilate themselves in the dazzling white of ecstasy—or of the Nocturnal Ascent of the Prophet during which he leaves behind, at each of the seven gates of the seven heavens, one of the essential coverings, *'anasir* [of the seven *lata'if* = *'anasir* = colored spiritual peri-elements between the body and the soul], of his created nature as the primordial Muhammadian Light.

Without confining oneself in art to the linear calligraphy of the letters of the Supreme Throne in the gray mist of incensings, the ultimate sign of the adoring presence of the predestined, the vocation of a Muslim country like Iraq should lead its artists to "resuscitate" by the use of the "couleur-lumière" the form of the interred Object in the "shroud" of the line; to attenuate the reliefs which would impaste with shadow the contours, to soften the irridescent light which must sustain the hues.

PART THREE

Gandhian Outlook and Techniques

Professor Louis Massignon:

Mr. Chairman, owing to official duties at the Paris University, it is only today, as Mr. Chairman said, that I am able to give my views before this Gandhian Seminar. There is a kind of earnestness in me because for many years I was concerned, not only intellectually but, I may say, spiritually and socially, with the Gandhian approach to a better order of things and behavior between men. As I have said in the summary I have given, I am beginning with the educational side of the Gandhian approach.

Usually one thinks that words have only tactical meaning and are slogans. In the case of Gandhi he did not use or invent such new words. He discovered the real meaning of the traditional words. He proceeded by a kind of interiorization: the fundamental way of thinking. When you have to learn something you must understand it. And how can you understand if you do not live with it so that it is a kind of engagement in meditation? I am not talking about mysticism, nor in an *ashram,* but I think that we cannot understand Gandhi, we cannot apply the ideas of Gandhi socially, if we have not meditated. It is not sufficient to learn. We must try to understand, and to understand, to keep in memory, you have to contemplate through words, the real meaning. That is the goal you must try to find.

In India, there is the question of vow—*vrata*. The point, I will say, after having studied this word, is that you meditate before getting into action, not merely by idealism. It means that

A talk presented to the Ministry of Education, New Delhi, January 7, 1953.

you are no longer theoretical; it means that you are steadfast, that you are meditating, contemplating. You are trying to find the inner meaning. You are fixed. You have woven your life. That goal was of great importance to Gandhiji. In 1929 all the people of the world agreed by the Kellogg Pact to live together in goodwill and peace. They all condemned war unconditionally. But they soon forgot the whole thing. Why? Because they did not meditate. Because they did not contemplate in accordance with the real meaning of the words, which is that we are striving for self-determination, to hold on in social work, to keep holding on, to realize that pledge. Omitting that, the pledge was forgotten.

Gandhi's life showed that his vow was that of a man who has contemplated the words that are used in his community for the religious approach. It is a question of sanctity, or sacredness. Dr. Kalelkar says *pavitra* or *punya*. But the sacredness is not realized personally by a vow of saintship. That is the great message of Gandhi.

We received from the Mahatma this great message of steadfastness in keeping a hold on truth. That is quite necessary and that is itself a part of *satyagraha*. The idea of satyagraha is the main point. As Professor Kabir said, Gandhiji at the end of his life knew things instinctively. He used words intuitively and not tactically. That is why he insisted particularly on individual satyagraha. It is only by personal steadfastness, by holding on to the pledge, the vow, that one may be useful to others. That is the way he waded through, crossed the river of life. That is the pilgrimage that makes people go to the sacred. Sacredness necessarily is among men. It is a question of the pledge of honor. It is impossible to live as a human being if you do not keep your word.

The next thing I will say, it is the last paragraph of my summary, concerns the question of heroism. It is very difficult for the masses to be heroic, but heroism for them remains necessary. Man's heroism is not insignificant. It is just as in therapeutics we have homeopathy — with a little drop we can change the world. Gandhi enjoined saintship for himself by losing everything, sacrificing for the community, using everyday common words whose meaning was lost to man but recovered by Gandhi.

At the end I would say that the leaders are not allowed the time to meditate. When they are in parliament, they have some sort of notes given by their secretaries, and that is practically what they answer. But if they were doing one or two hours of meditation, before the discussion on the main point, not merely judging as barristers, but as souls living in this world, then they would be able to answer the questions rightfully. Gandhi himself was a barrister, but a barrister for the sake of truth, not tactically. He grasped the principle and was using it in his fight in South Africa. That was the beginning of satyagraha. He brought steadfastness by using common words for justice and truth. These had been badly used as traps for fools but are also a pledge for saints to keep their vows. They are also used by the masses so that we can immediately make the people understand.

We must make this clear especially to those who are holding power, those who are leading in the U.S. – excuse me Mr. Bunche, but I think that we must induce them by some means to consider these aspects of truth, because, otherwise, there may come the eventuality of a third war. Nobody wants it, but the emergency may arise. In that case, we must at least hold on to the idea that there may be zones of security, for hospitals, for the wounded, for refugees, and for shrines and artistic monuments. They must not be exposed to the atom bomb and the gas. That is perfectly unbearable. We must insist on enforcing the Geneva convention (cf. *Revue Internationale de la Croix-Rouge*, Geneva, June 1952, pp. 449–468). We must get all the nations to sign an agreement for having, in cases of emergency, protected places for hospitals and the wounded. There should be no indiscriminate use of bombs and gas. That would be horrible.

The second thing is to make all the people share the same privileges. That is, create zones of security for refugees, for displaced persons. This will be work for the ideal of truth and justice. We must ask all the governments to have zones of security in their territories, to have homes for the refugees. If it is necessary for some people to get out of their countries, they should not be treated brutally. We should have the old principle, the old Indian principle that is written in the *Manava Dharma Shastra*—the idea of the *atithi*—of hospitality to the guest; the *caranya dharma* or the right of protection for the man who is a refugee, as for the Buddhist mendicant. Asking for this protection was a sacred right among the Buddhists. If we could grasp the full meaning of this old Indian principle, and also get others to share it, then something could be done.

I was yesterday at Mehrauli and visited Kutbuddin Bakhtyar's shrine. Gandhiji, as you know, visited it—it was his last pilgrimage, four days before his death, together with some Muslim ladies of Delhi, who had (at the instance of Bibi Amat-al-Salam) shared his last fasting and broken it with him. He found the shrine damaged, promised to have it repaired (this promise was fulfilled in 1950 as stated by an Arabic inscription), prayed with the worshippers, vowed with them a pledge of brotherhood, that Delhi might solve the problem of unity of India through nonviolence. But four days later, he was killed. It was his last social act; he wanted to make unity between Indians, between Hindus and Muslims. It was a sacred place for Muslims. He wanted to atone for others, for his brethren who had broken the shrine.

If it would be possible to force UNESCO and the U.N., in their deliberations, to decide that sacred places should be respected, it would be a great achievement. There was a conference in Amsterdam two years ago and it was decided there that artistic monuments and shrines should be privileged, because they are sacred places. They are places of *pavitra* or *punya*. A sacred place is a place where people think of God, try to find *moksha*, to find a way out from this base world, to go to God. It must be insisted that if there must be zones of security for the wounded, zones of security for refugees in case of emergency of war, there must be zones for the sacred places also, as artistic and beautiful places are places where people go for the contemplation of God.

Now, I will make a fuller explanation of my points.

I will first deal with my personal approach to the Gandhian mission. In 1921, thirty years ago, I was a young professor of Muslim sociology at the Paris University. The university was visited by Dr. Ansari and Professor Suleiman Nadvi, who were the heads of the pro-Khilafat Commission in Paris. They gave me the satyagraha pledge of Gandhi. It was published in *Revue du Monde Musulman* in April 1921, showing its main accordance with Islam. It was through Muslims that I knew Gandhi and I understood the ideal of Gandhi, the ideal of satyagraha, the pursuit of truth by steadfastness in will, by *vrata*, by oath. I also learned through Dr. Abdul Majid that satyagraha was a sacred thing for the Muslims also. I realized immediately that there was something in Gandhi which was valuable. For perhaps the first time in the world, there was a man having influence on people of other religions with great social results.

Atithi dharma is one of the fundamentals in the Laws of Manu. From it derives the right of sanctuary, which is found also in Islam. I was saved in Iraq among the Montafiq Arabs by *atithi dharma* some forty-four years ago. I was an archaeologist working there and was denounced as a spy. Unfortunately many Europeans were often in the Intelligence Service. I was not in the Intelligence Service, but I was supposed to be in it and therefore thought to be a spy. I was taken prisoner and was going to be killed. But I had been the guest of a noble family. The head of the family said to the people who were taking me, "If you kill Massignon you will be killing one of ourselves. He is our guest and a guest is a sacred thing. You cannot therefore kill him. You know that he is our guest and therefore he is the guest of God and you must not touch him." I know that in India too it is a very sacred principle. Even among the most savage tribal people, the guest is sacred. So I was saved by the ideal of the right of sanctuary, the *caranya dharma*. I can never forget that.

This very spring I was among the Montafiq Arabs again, with my wife, and I told her what Emir Adil Arslan had said to the first U.N. meeting in Paris. There was a widow of a bedouin chief, whose husband had been killed. One night, at the approach to a tent she saw a man who was a fugitive, who came and took hold of a string of the tent. Among the Arabs, if you hold the string of the tent, you are sacred, you are a guest. So she welcomed him and gave three days' safety to the guest. After that she allowed him to escape, though he was the murderer of her husband. I do not say she forgave him. I only say that she stood steadfast to the ideal of the right of sanctuary. We in Europe have lost the sense of the sacred in social life, but through people like Gandhi we can regain it. In India people were in agreement with him in the cause of right of sanctuary. We have to make the people of the world take to this principle, that the guest is of God and that his right is higher than war, even just war. In India the masses still believe in it. It may be said that if we can work on this principle, we can make peace stand over war, we can have war killed. We can kill war only by the right of sanctuary. We should see that the foreigner is not considered a spy, should believe that he is not acting to betray us. In Europe we do not have the steadfastness or the hope that the guest may be really of God. We are afraid the guest may be of the Devil, that he may be a spy, of the Intelligence Service, and too often it happens so. That is one reason why most of the Eastern people are fed up with European peoples, who break their pledge as easily as they give it.

From 1921 onward I was working with some Frenchmen, trying to see how the Satyagraha Pledge of Truth could be made to capture the French mind. By mixing with the masses, Gandhi was able to influence them. In India you do not keep spiritual and material things apart. They are integrated. That is not the case in Europe. We keep the spiritual aside from the temporal.

In December, 1931, Gandhi came to Paris and I had the privilege to meet him twice. One of us asked him: "How and in what way could religion help in advocating the suppression of war?" Gandhi very simply answered: "Official religions are very weak for stopping war." Of course official religions have the support of the state. They have the material goods, they have the material prosperity, so that they are very weak in spiritual matters. When a state enters into a war, they could call it a just war and ask everyone to be prepared to die for that country. The people have not taken the satyagraha pledge, and therefore they have to go the way the state asks them to go.

I was very much impressed by this talk with Gandhi. We French attempted to publish a little periodical called *Nouvelles de L'Inde*—News from India. But it was not much of a success. We could not get the support of bankers. Mrs. Guieysse, the founder, did not have the privilege to find rich friends for this social action. I was, however, much interested by the possibility of pilot cells of action. These I would call operative cells. I think Gandhi's ideals are quite fit to make little cells, little pilot cells in different European centers, where people, who are united by such pledges—not secret pledges like Masonic pledges, but pledges with free determination or vow—could stand together. A man who has vowed the pledge would not like to break the pledge. It is not an oath, because an oath is from outside, from below. In the case of pledge, you pledge willingly. A pledge is from inside. It is the realization in your life. When you vow a pledge you are united with a definite ideal.

By educating people to take the satyagraha pledge, you can gradually make people understand the spiritual power, the power of the soul. Acharya Kripalani said that it was gradually and slowly that Gandhi became acquainted with this weapon of satyagraha. He moulded the world only after practicing the thing himself. Here is a booklet by Gandhi. It is called *From Yeravda Mandir*. It contains in English the quintessence of the Gandhian soul. There are so many remarkable counsels in this book. It is a spiritual book. I went to some of the leading booksellers here to get a copy of this book. It was a surprise to me to know that a copy was not available anywhere. I was shocked. Herbert translated this book. We are also making a book on nonviolent philosophy. It is going to be published soon. It is a textbook for making people understand the nonviolent technique. Professor Meile and Professor Lacombe, who are interested in seeing the works of Gandhi published, have cooperated in this endeavor. I think we cannot get into action until we have grasped the meaning, until we have steadfastness. We must follow the way of Gandhi. That is the meaning of pilgrimage. We must go on his way. We must try to understand his words, because his words were not empty words, but words born of his personal experience. We must very closely study his words. Many of them are summaries of his experiences, explained in common words, in words we understand. That is the social value of meditation and contemplation before action. If I insisted on it at the beginning, it is because the beginning of action is contemplation. That is what Gandhi has proved. I do not know if Professor Kripalani could explain at what time Gandhi used to take to meditation.

Acharya Kripalani:

While he was acting he was meditating.

Professor Massignon:

Is it so? In the performance of his every act he was meditating? I understand Gandhi's meditation was always directed towards social action and it was his immediate goal. We must understand that it is impossible to perform a social action without a kind of vow. It is determination. It is the determination to suffer any consequences, good or bad, in the performance of that action. What is a hunger-strike? Gandhi said, "It is not a technique to coerce others to your way of action. It is a desire coming from God that obliges me to hunger-strike." Till the end of his life he was forbidding some of his followers to undertake hunger-strikes. It was distasteful for him to make fasting a weapon. So this question of understanding the true meaning of certain Sanskrit words Gandhi chose is very important in order to understand his actions. In the program of this seminar we talk of tensions. I do not know what is the Indian word for *tension*. What is the Sanskrit word for *tension*? Do you know, Professor Kripalani?

Acharya Kripalani:

I do not know. You may ask Kakh Kalelkar.

Professor Massignon:

Do you know Mr. Kalelkar?

Kakh Kalelkar:

Conflict . . . *Sangharshana.*

Professor Massignon:

There are not only bad tensions, there are tensions for good, for justice. Satyagraha is also a tension, a tension for a good cause. It was slowly and by experimenting in his beliefs that this young barrister gained stature in his spiritual personality. If we read Gandhi's works, written in English, and carefully watch the words he chose to use in them, we find that Tolstoy and Ruskin had a great influence on this man. He also maintained his faith in prayer and the native value of Sanskrit words in Gujrati. His commentary on the *Gita* is full of spiritual meaning and value. No doubt he acquired most of his knowledge through the medium of a foreign language, through the English language, but he always attached the greatest value to the native and pure meaning of the old Sanskrit words for justice and truth. Let us examine their meaning as felt by Gandhi. We are surprised, for instance, when he says that God is *satya;* God is truth. It implies all the metaphysics. God is Satya because we know that He is Truth, when we read it in English, but he also knew that it has social significance. The greatest metaphysicians in India had said it is the essence of God. "God is the essence of vow," Gandhi said, because He is Truth, in social realizations.

We must therefore realize the full meaning of the extensive use of Sanskrit words by Gandhi. We must go into the native value of certain of these words that were said in India in Sanskrit. We among Europeans are anxious to see that you Gandhists in India understand correctly the significance of the words often uttered by Gandhi and help us follow them as best as possible. I am now speaking to the Indian Gandhists. You have not tried sufficiently to bring home to your conservative isolationists the meaning of Gandhi's preachings. You have not exercised sufficiently your mind to show them that Gandhi belonged to the purest Aryan tradition, that he had grasped the fundamentals of the Sanskrit texts (his commentary on the *Gita* bears testimony to this); that he placed himself in truth alone; that Gandhi has not betrayed the law of the Indian community and that he has kept the oath.

It is not an oath, necessarily, in the literal sense of the Sanskrit word, which in the Law of Manu states, "They will keep it at all costs." He kept the oath in the sense that through his atonement he found social compassion for the masses. The masses are illiterate. They are not responsible for the narrowness of conservative leaders because they are simple men. You have got to impress upon the Indian conservatives that Gandhi did not do anything which went against their *dharma;* on the other hand, that their creed was maintained and enriched by Gandhi. As you all know, he died uttering the words *"Ram Ram."* They were the last words on his lips.

Unlike many, Gandhi had realized the meaning of his utterances and that mantras were meant to be practiced. He was a believer in the universal brotherhood of man. He had equal respect for pure faith in all religions and cultures. In short, he knew no barriers between one human being and another. Naturally, to understand the world outside India, he had to fall back on the English language and he did not regard that as a sin. His mission was the unification of Mother India. He wished for the integration of all religious units who have a common culture and tradition.

With this teaching of Gandhi in mind, how can you help us in getting out of war? In a general Satyagraha? "You will be defeated in diplomatic action," says the doubter and the skeptic. This however is the counsel of a foreigner or guest to the Indian Gandhist. Gandhi believed in the potential power of satyagraha so much that he employed it right through his fight against the foreign rule in India.

Truth is also in Arabic, *haqq*. This concept is very important for Muslims. Among them you have the memorial of a saint of Baghdad, Mansur Hallaj, "who died for truth." He is named in Bengali "Satyapir," the master of truth. This memorial unites Indian *satya* and Muslim *haqq* in a practical worshipping of truth, socially acting (according to Professor Muhyiuddin of Dacca whom I met in Montreal) in Faridpur (Sureswara) and Chittagong (Maij Bhandar). In two places he visited in Chittagong you still have people that are worshipping *satya* or truth. Those who believe that life is to be sacrificed for truth's sake, whether Muslim or Hindu, live by truth.

In the true meaning, his life becomes really a fulfilled oath, for it is a vow, a *vrata*. Vow has a very important role to play in our everyday life, but at the present time it is ignored. Without the vow, how can we have any attachment to the work that we undertake and how can we be sincere in fulfilling the tasks? Vow is not meant to be against the law. It accomplishes the law. It is not against *dharma;* it is an accomplishment of *dharma*. Gandhi never wanted his followers to be timid while fulfilling their vows. He wanted them to possess all the qualities of a hero.

Another aspect of satyagraha is pilgrimage. It means that you may cross the water, *tirtha,* to leave your goods, to leave your common goods. It is a kind of sacrifice. There are places like Hardwar and Banaras and so on. It is in a pilgrimage toward Truth that Gandhi went to all such places, wherever they exist. It was not in any sense of complacency. Sacrifice is still the meaning of the pilgrimage for the man who has a vow of *satya*. Among the Hindus there is a common belief of going to *moksha* in the way in which the Muslims think of going to Mecca, which is not something material but something spiritual like the *moksha* of the Hindus. Gandhiji never failed to keep in touch with the people by going on a pilgrimage with others and that was for realization of his vow. Yesterday, when I was on Gandhiji's track at Mehrauli, I realized that if he made a Muslim pilgrimage there, he did this for the sake of compassion towards

Muslims, as he understood that Muslims were truly Indians. This is a very important thing in the life of Gandhiji. It does not mean that he surrendered to the Muslims, but it shows his compassion for them. He understood that there was something common and very deep between Muslims and Hindus in India and that Truth should be worked in social practice.

On the eve of his death, Gandhiji had written that seven hundred thousand villages in India were not properly organized and that social corporate life of India must depend upon the unity and the organization of these villages. There must be satyagraha in each village for universal brotherhood. People of differing creeds live in the same village, eat the same food and work together. He thought that there was a possibility of social corporate life.

The last two years of Gandhi's life are very important. In these two years, if one goes through his editorials in the *Harijan,* one can see horrible happenings taking place, people killing one another, and doing all sorts of heinous things. Gandhiji took the blame on himself and said, "I have been a bad workman." He did not use words lightly like so many of us, but realized their full meaning and resorted to satyagraha to atone for others' sins.

Now I will comment upon the word *tension.* It is difficult to translate it in Sanskrit. The most common of the tensions is towards war. Tensions generally mean an opposition to something, but satyagraha is an exception to it as it is tension for holding on to Truth.

I was in Chicago last October. I met a man there doing social work for a hundred thousand refugees from Lithuania and Poland. He was a Jew. Mr. Saul Alinsky. It is very interesting to know about him and his activities. He says love for most people is merely a feeling, a weak feeling and that we must have a tension for justice and truth and a tension for making refugees realize them. He gave the refugees an idea of a better life in claiming full civic rights for them. This man, Alinsky, was doing Gandhian work, though unaware of it, among refugees. We must understand that somebody has to take a satyagraha pledge. It is a word of honor and not any ordinary thing and we must keep to it. This is the real meaning of satyagraha and we must make it known through UNESCO to all the world. Another important thing is that people who were persecuted found an asylum in India—for instance, the Parsis. This is all due to the deep feeling of the sacredness of the guest in India.

When I visited Alinsky's field of activity in Chicago, I found something Gandhian. When I told the American Committee of Social Thought about this, somebody said that this man was going to the masses and behaving as a Communist. We investigated into the matter and found that he was a man full of tension for justice, including justice for the masses. We found that it was not at all Communism he preached but an old powerful truth. Pursuing the truth is not belonging to a party.

I feel something has to be done in America by this Gandhian technique if we are to resolve the many tensions there. Gandhi's method is not intellectual but spiritual. We are obliged to look for a ray of hope from personalities like the Mahatma. It is impossible to know the masses by merely intellectual means. I do not know that there is any contradiction between the intellectual and spiritual aspects of Gandhiji. What I mean is that there is something deeper than the intellect in Gandhiji. His life is of the spiritual mold and not of the intellectual mold. As Professor Kripalani said, Gandhi was not a genius intellectually, but he was a moral genius. It was he who understood the world. He did not care about dogmas and philosophies. He cared more about purity in manner and behavior. He did not wish to have a philosophy of his own. His was the old philosophy.

For birth control, Gandhiji advocated *brahmacharya vrata* or celibacy even in family life. What medical men talk of birth control is taken from statistics. Gandhiji in his autobiography has given a true exposition of his vow of *brahmacharya vrata*.

You might have read how on the very eve of his death he drafted a note on the organization of municipal life in India. He said that if there be in every village a number of men wedded to the satyagraha pledge, in the long run India would be one and it would be really a Mother India for the world.

I had the honor of sitting in an international conference recently and I was talking to my neighbor. This man said that people are slow to recognize that better distribution of land would make people averse to wars. They were having statistics after statistics in the U.N., but here in India they have started redistribution of land voluntarily, under an inspired leader, Mr. Vinoba Bhave. They realize the design of justice. It is perfectly possible to live in even a crowded world if the ideas of the Food and Agriculture Organization as stated in its reports are molded in this fashion. We are trying for rational distribution of land, but most people only say we shall begin, but do not want to sacrifice. This is the main problem in India. I think the idea of having land given to labor and the ploughmen voluntarily by owners, by the landowners, is called the *sarvodaya*. I request you to convey this idea to the Food and Agriculture Organization, through this Gandhi Seminar. This would be a contribution of India to the F.A.O. UNESCO also ought to take more interest in this idea.

As for the question of refugees, *caranarthi*, there should be an international law for the refugees. At the last U.N. conference in Paris, a note of ours, through Professor Dehousse, who attended as an official delegate, stated that there must be zones of security for refugees in case of the emergency of a new war. It is unsound, it is degrading to denationalize the refugees. In the United States, the refugees have to become Americans, learn their language and become American citizens, and then, as they say, they will have the rights. They are saving themselves to the detriment of the future. These people are therefore made to forget their culture. Take the case of Lithuanians. They have even forgotten their language. In some cases, they might like to come back. Their country might be liberated. It is acting wrongly to force them to give up their own nationality. These refugees are the guests of God. They should remain Lithuanians. I have seen even more horrible things. The Volkdeutscher Germans become American citizens and are sent back, armed with weapons to fight against Eastern Germany. They are welcome to take American citizenship, but is it their duty to take weapons and fight their own nationals for the safety of America?

But why should they not be considered as refugees? The U.N. does not yet consider them so. India has still this problem. There are thousands of Muslims crossing the border of Rajputana every month. Similarly there are still millions of Hindus living uneasily in Eastern Pakistan. They are separated because of the supposed incompatibility of their cultures. Here I have a book in Devanagri script written by a Muslim from Dacca. This man has much more of the real Indian culture than many Hindus. Forgive me for talking of these things as a foreigner, as a Westerner, but I think they show the ultimate unity of India. To force a people out of their land is horrible, because it is against justice, it is against truth. Muslims in Eastern Pakistan are Indians, Bengalis. I think, Sir, that refugees must not be denationalized and forced to adopt the nationality of the country in which they seek refuge. We have lost the sense of sacredness. We have lost the sense of Gandhi, who was the last of the saints.

In the search of the intellect for the truth, we do not yet realize that science must be disinterested. We are breaking heads with science. I am acknowledged as professor at the University of Paris, but I am not allowed to share with a foreign visiting professor the power of examining our common students for their doctorates. This is silly. You give him the power of teaching, but not the power of assessing the values. At other universities I get many more privileges than I do in France itself. On this question of supernationalization, forgive me if I refer again to the Kutbuddin shrine. I have been deeply touched by Gandhiji's social work, and I think this disinterested action was his best message. I feel here was real supernationalism. This is a very important thing in Gandhi, in Nehru, and in Maulana Abul Kalam Azad.

The great thing is to contemplate through social work. The aim must be *moksha*. That must be by the vow. One must feel through the vow the sacredness of God. It is not merely intellectual, but a spiritual realization. God is not an invention. God is a discovery. You must forgive me if I mention my personal point of view, because it is the main idea of Gandhi that the person is important. On the social point of view, it is a perpetual problem—this satyagraha. Whether in 1921, 1931, or

1948, it was for Gandhi exactly the same, the same spiritual idea. Today the problem of satyagraha is to make a new application of Gandhi's spiritual strength so that there may be a new evocation of the spirit on a wide scale.

From the days I was very young, I was longing for India. For the second time, I am now visiting India. India has always cast a spell over me. God hides himself in a way. We have to find him. *Iswara* hides in us. We are his shrine. It is only when the shrine is broken that the perfume of his presence is revealed. We have to make sacrifices. You find that in the text of the *Vedas* and the *Brahamanas*. I felt most that Gandhi had always tried to console the brokenhearted. The brokenhearted recognized in him one who would help them truly and efficiently. Men in their misery went to him and got help and guidance. Gandhi was a man of sorrow, and it is only the man of sorrow who discovers God. He discovers Him in the humble weavers, in the nakedness of the untouchables. By becoming naked himself, he tries to make their sorrows clothed.

The Transfer of Suffering
through Compassion
(1959)

I

Everyone of us has been acquainted with queer cases of "transfer" of pain even of moral evil: of suffering felt (not only *of,* but) *from* others' woes or misdeeds. This transfer hurts often unconscious, innocent, or irresponsible beings, arousing physical and mental illnesses. Psychoanalysts, through the investigation of dreams, try to cure the mind of such "traumatisms," mere unuseful "remains" of old forgotten "shocks"; – in showing to the patient that they originated from inaccurately "intentionalized" and "personalized" former "misunderstandings." No real good should be anticipated, they say, from others' illnesses, whatever homeopathic osmosis of compassion may be fancied.

Nevertheless, sociologists have to face cases where "dreams" of compassion led interference in the events of social life, when men, obviously convinced that they must, at all costs, "realize" such a compassion, do keep their "pledge" to others, to foreigners, styled as their adopted "guests of honor." Sociologists, digging with Frazer the earth of mythical folklore, try to cure the ambient society of such foolish "potlatches," of such "extravagant" prodigality of "human wealth," showing that it is plain madness to lay claim for an impossible "transfer" of a penalty before any sound tribunal, human or divine, and that the trespassers should be punished for this insolence towards the law.

155

Promethean rebels are to be scourged. Moral virtue is a "middle" between two excesses, and nothing else.

II

But we are induced to investigate more deeply the matter. Common sense makes "conscientious objections," and observes that transmissive compassion has been historically ascertained, in heroic lives, that "Hero worship" is the positive basis of history, which recent thinkers have wrongly reduced to unconscious and impersonal conflicts between mere abstractions, laws (rational) or archetypes (irrational), or mere slogans. The impact of "heroic compassion" on most of our human, traditional, and legendary records (and legend is an immediate projection of the event in the world of symbols), shows that there is *the secret of history,* and that this secret is disclosed only to an elite, tested only by men of sorrow and compassion, born to assume the blind anguish of living multitudes and to understand and announce its transcendental glory.

Among the myriads of anonymous sufferers, helplessly crushed and so quickly forgotten, apparently unavenged, it is enough, for justice offended, to rely on the faithful hope that, intermittently, a hero of compassion may appear, from the midst of wars and plagues, as the herald of a doomsday for all, as unexceptionable as unavoidable.[1]

But how begins this vocation for heroic compassion? By an *"épochè,"* by a sudden stop of time, by a sudden abolition of space, by a shock, psychosomatic, viz., in the heart of someone passing by, on the common road. Someone who suddenly perceives, on the side of his path, a beggar standing, or a wounded, or a dying wretch, a single case of blind despair. Someone who has an instant of mindedness, better than a thousand years of nursing administratively, mechanically, and deceivedly, as do "benevolent societies." It is a sparkle from some unknown personal being, badly veiled under the wretch's poverty, fleshing out the holes of this pierced frock of disabled humanity. A

Fire, quickening the careless heart with an everlasting Need. Gautama on his royal youth's road, the Good Samaritan going down on his tradesway. The psychosomatic shock they endured was deeper than human love; it was absolute desire defying the lack of justice in the whole world, a kind of revolt against the laws of nature, in the name of their hidden Lawgiver; "in the Name of the Compassionate," as says the beginning of the Muslim prayer.

That kind of temptation has begun in humanity, after the ambivalent shock of the first sex appeal: with the awful woe of children when deprived of their fathers by death, looking on the corpses not only with suspicious fear of an uncleanliness, as Frazer (and Graham Greene) sums it up, but with cryptical hope of a purifying sacralization. They had not chosen them.

Such is the paradoxical way for the "phenomenal appearance," in this world, of the spiritual, Absolute, of religion, as postulated by Professor Y. Moroi. Not only for men, through men. But also for all living beings, from men, through humanity; wherever she is shining with the virginally feminine smile of pity, as a mirror; in whatever Ise pilgrims may seek it.

In a powerful work entitled *The Roots of Heaven* (which the Far East may understand easier than our West), Romain Gary tells us the tale of "The prisoners and the beetles." Prisoners are suffering badly in a concentration camp, helplessly crushed. When they see, at their feet, on the ground, some flying beetles overthrown, hopelessly on their backs, unable to stand and fly again. At once, some of the prisoners (from the political section; those of the "common law" remain blind), realize the emergency, and strive, and stoop, to put again the beetles standing on their legs. It sounds so silly, but it is obeying that unwritten law which shall free us from every material jail.

It doesn't open immediately, but it shows the way of escape, as the "mental decentering" of Copernicus escaping from the Ptolemaic universe. And it is an experimental discovery, not an "a priori" invented synthetical axiomatic.

To be genuine, in itself, this absolute psychosomatic shock must create a permanent link between us and the object of our compassion and cooperate in the building of mankind's unity.

Statistical parapsychology shows, in thousands of cases of telepathy and precognition, how this link is "constellated" and built,[2] how every one of us, without having the slightest propension to heroism, is "mobilized" by suffering for others' sake. And that it holds on for true progress of true welfare. The history of humanity is "overstreaming" (specially in Japan) with positive and fruitful experiments of "transmissive compassion." And for something else than material aims, if through material means, in family, mankind, friendship.

If these cases have been underrated and neglected during centuries of scientific research, it is because their *parapsychological genuineness* had not been discriminated from the administrative tricks of too manly priesthoods, which indulged in torturing self-denying souls, as surgeons do with "guinea pigs." And also because most of these silent bearers of the wounds of "transmissive compassion," being women, did not attempt to complain and speak, keeping in their hearts the divine secret. But now rises on the world the star of the promotion of the Immaculate Woman, foreseen by Gandhi in Sita and Savitri; and not in Asia only; of Fatimat al-Batul, in Islam,[3] as of Mary, in Christianity: with her apparitions increasingly dazzling, since 1830, from Paris to La Salette, and from Lourdes to Fatima.

III

Here below, some documents on premonitorial *dreams* linked to their objective *"answers."* (N.B.: the first shock, being unconnected with ordinary life, looks like a dream, as long as the objective fulfilling does not "awake" the witness: see Peter in Acts 11:6–11.)

The premonitorial *dream* gives the picture of usual things as a symbol for spiritual realities; and the *answer* makes the witness grasp at the spiritual reality in recovering the material presence of the usual things alluded to.

1. About the *shroud*. Muslim dreams of a shroud normally

mean friendly prayers comforting the soul of the deceased, wrapping her under this mantle:

a. *The desire for a shroud* (Istanbul, Aug. 1945). I was coming back from my friend Omar Fevzi Mardin (in Scutari) when a young Turkish physician who had recently lost a friend, told me: "I had felt summoned" to go, and remain alone at the side of the corpse; I was seized by a silent awe, about which I kept secret. Later on my wife told me she had dreamt of another of my friends who had also died a premature death and said to her in her dream: "Do tell your husband to wrap me with the same white shroud he used with his first deceased friend." From where did this dream come to her?

b. *The removal of the shroud* (Qarafa, Cairo, May 9, 1937). A very pure Muslim Shadhili nun, Nabiha Wafa'iya (d. 1934) said in a dream to a friend (H.Q.), the night before the removal of her corpse (to a new tomb): "Don't remain troubled about me; you shall find my body incorrupt, because I never did anything implying dissolution." And the body was found incorrupt and flexible, naked, *without* her shroud of 1934. I have prayed here on January 15, 1959 with Hasan Qasim, SE. from Masjid Fathallah Bannānī.

2. About the *sweat* (by Fear of God) (Qarafa, Cairo, circa 1041). In this cemetery, from the tomb of the "Bride of the Desert" ('Arus al-Sahra), sweat, as a balm, used to ooze, curing pilgrims of their soul and body diseases. It was the "sweat of agony" which had seized a young girl, the daughter of the Muhaddith Abulhasan Ibn Ghalbun, on the eve of her nuptial night, when going to be unveiled by her betrothed she had prayed, "O God, prevent any creature from seeing my nakedness," and suddenly fell dead.[4] Her tomb was still extant in 1773 (according to Gawhar Sukkari, *Kawkab sā'ir*), between Imam Layth and Fakhr Farisi.

3. *The witnessing of the blood* (Kerbela, Irak, circa 1510). When Shah Ismail visited the tombs of the martyrs killed together with Husayn (in 680), where this grandson of the Prophet had risen for the sake of the honor of Islam, stained by a dissolute ruler, he stopped before the tomb of Imam Hurr Tamimi

and was told that he was not a martyr, having been commissioned by the bad ruler to induce Husayn to fall in the trap where he was killed. Shah Ismail ordered the disinterment of the corpse, and before destroying it, attempted to remove from his forehead the frontlet Husayn himself had put there, to honor Imam Hurr (who, as soon as he had realized how treacherously he had been made use of against Husayn, had asked his forgiveness, and turned back against the besiegers, charging them until he was killed); the blood ran afresh from the forehead, and Shah Ismail, struck with remorse, ordered that a cupola be built on the tomb, which I visited twice, 1908, 1953.[5] Preternatural justification suits the unjustly distrusted witness Imam Hurr's witnessing for Husayn remains, while Muktar's awful revenge taken on the murderers of Husayn has not outlived him.

One may find at length the wide belief, in Muslim countries, concerning the witnessing of Husayn Mansur Hallaj's blood (crucified Baghdad, 922), in the study given by Rawan Farhadi (*Revue des Etudes Islamiques,* Paris, 1955, pp. 69–91); and of his ashes, swallowed, either by virgins or by the doves of the minaret from where they were spread in the air; still I was told in February 1908 that these doves were cooing "*haqq,* truth," in remembrance of the martyr (see the *Encyclopédie de la Musique,* Fasquelle, Paris, I [1958], pp. 77–82).

The same witnessing of the blood is to be found in Christianity with the link between the "thrust of the lance" at Calvary, and the stigmatization of St. Francis and others. And, without bloodshed, in the visions of Muslim mystics concerning the "opening of the breast" (*sharh al-sadr*) such as of the Prophet Muhammad.

I must now add two evidences, not only personal but direct, on "transmissive compassion":

a. *Fasting for peace in justice.* Coming back from Washington, where I had thought about Lincoln's fasting for the sake of the black slaves, and from Mehrauli (South of New Delhi), where I had meditated about the last fasting of Gandhi, I had realized in France, in the summer of 1953, that some evil deeds performed against Muslims by some of my countrymen, most of them Christians, were staining the spiritual purity of our common spiritual body, of our dear Motherland, Joan of Arc's Motherland. Accordingly, I joined with some friends in atoning for our brethren going astray, acting as if we were "substituted" for these ill-treated Muslims. We were fasting periodically, specially during Ramadan, the lunar month of Muslim "Lent." Several Muslims, touched, joined us in prayer. One of them openly struggled with me to make joint Muslim-Christian pilgrimages, visit such common places of worship as the Seven Sleepers of Ephesus (ahl al-kahf) in Vieux Marché (France), and Guidjel (near Setif, Algeria). And one day, this friend, Professor Hajj Lounis Mahfoud wrote to me, it was on April 25, 1957, that on the next night, 27th of Ramadan, the most solemn Night of Destiny, when we were to pray specially for Muslims' sake, he would also "communicate" with us by compassion, praying for our common spiritual goal at the Cemetery of the Seven Sleepers in Guidjel ("alone, not compromising anybody"); on June 5 next, he was killed; as a sacralized victim; I was myself exposed twice to murderous attacks, showing the reality of our spiritual compassion for Peace's sake, as Gandhi's and Lincoln's deaths did.

b. *Atoning for a lack of filial duty.* On August 30, 1958, it was granted to me to come and bow, in dutiful recollection, before a Japanese friend's grave (R. Adm. Y. Sh., d. February 28, 1942), together with his son, at Aoyama Boshi, Tokyo—in fulfillment of an ancient "covenant of friendship." He had made me confidant of a deep secret sorrow (Paris, June 9, 1921) endured since that day of 1917, in Hong Kong, when he had heard of the death of his father. He suffered not only because he had not been able to attend the funeral in Tokyo, but because he had religiously "renounced" performance of the normal duty of a Japanese son toward his ancestors; and he had left me an atoning "ex-voto" to be exposed, in a definite place of worship, in Paris, for all the Japanese forefathers and their descendants (at St. Antoine).

Six months later, I had most unexpectedly to endure the same suffering at my father's death (January 18, 1922:[6] two hours after

I had made, for the father of a friend in spiritual need, the same filial "renunciation" (as R. Adm. Y. Sh.). The last, and perhaps strangest "parapsychological encounter" occurred for me last June, when at last my Japanese friend's ex-voto was, after thirty-seven years negotiations, officially and safely exposed at the very place he desired. And it coincided with a letter from the Japanese Organizing Committee of the Congress in Tokyo, telling me, on June 6, 1958, that "after careful consideration," he had "decided to accept my application to read a paper at the forthcoming Congress for the History of Religions." And this was done, on August 28, at 16 h. 30.

IV

From the above documentation may be inferred how to "spot" the threshold of sacralization (*pavitra, punya*): in an *"overstretched"* trial of painful love, in a "hyperextension" of self for mental identification with the other's need; when one cannot help him, except by sharing, mentally, so poorly, his pain. By tears, if one can't afford blood—by the burning of his hunger, if one's breast can't give him the milk of human kindness? Tears and blood, milk and fire are the means of the housekeeping, of the immemorial rite of hospitality and the rite of asylum (*atithi dharma, caranya dharma*). But they are undiscoverable and unworkable if one has not "recovered his mother's womb" in pilgrimage, bound straight in his own hospitality for others, by the pledge of honor which alone may render "lawful" the bread, render "apportionable" in common the truth (*satya*), sought on the same path.

Here lies the ford, the wade (*tirtha*), for crossing—from parapsychological research to the invisible realm. Here we get on from the "orderly" material world, through a distortion (Einsteinian) of Space *and* Time to an "overorderly," chronogrammatically personalized "constellation" of human events: no longer causalized, but as Jung says, "synchronized" by their intelligible meaning; which appears *apotropaic,* i.e., transmissible—not genealogically, but as a chain of spiritual rings.

There, in apotropaic sacralization, through transmissive compassion, do we meet the metaphysical problem of what may be the *link;* between these rings in this chain? Externally, it looks like *karma,* like a mere transmigration of souls, moved by the Wheel of Destiny. But, from inside, in the personal begetting of one's own vow (*vrata*), it is felt as escape, thanks to a hook, an anchor, sent to save our hearts—as from a star, from above.

I shall be very short on the kinship between these experimental data, on "transmissive compassion" from soul to soul, and the theory of the *"transmigration of souls."* I have studied it only among Muslims of the extreme Shi'ite tendency; for them, every man has only one single soul, and it can be easily suggested that "transmigration" among Muslim Shi'a is akin to the transhistoric inspiration of the Spirit which is transmitted from the founder of a religious order to his successor generation after generation, just as from Elias as far as John the Baptist. While in Indonesia, the Spirit which "inspires," the Sumangat, doesn't transmigrate—and the transmigration is reserved to the seven or nine minor souls which constitute the personality of the individual soul for every man or woman. This dislocation of the polyvalent soul in the Far East looks like a punishment, her *karma;* because all the spiritual progress under the inspiration of the Spirit of Holiness leads towards unification of the individual soul through ascetical training, sacrifice, and compassion, to Unity.

Concerning the last, not least, problem of human compassion, towards *suffering animals*—misunderstood by such Westerners as Descartes—the best has been said by Léon Bloy (*La Femme pauvre [The Woman Who Was Poor]*, 86–116) and Romain Gary (*Les Racines du ciel [The Roots of Heaven]*, 196, 433); cosmic unanimity ends there.

NOTES

1. See my communication on substitution (in Arabic: *badaliya*) through compassion, at the Alexandria meeting of the Continuing Committee for Muslim-Christian Cooperation (Feb. 9, 1955; trans-

lated in French in *L'Ame populaire,* Paris, June 1955, no. 321; cf. Anne Fremantle, in *The Commonweal,* Aug. 9, 1957, pp. 466–468). And *Badaliya bulletin XI.*

2. Researches of Prof. Gotthard Booth (Columbia University) and of Prof. Rhine (Duke University, North Carolina).

3. See *Eranos Jahrbücher* 24 (Zurich, 1956), pp. 119–132.

4. See *Bull. Inst. Fr. Archeol. Or.* 57 (Cairo, 1957), pp. 55, 87.

5. See Mamuqani, *Tanqih al-maqāl* (Tehran, 1952), p. 260.

6. My father's "modeled prints" and gilded eglomisations had been strongly influenced by Japanese art; see my "impressions on Ise" for the deep impression of the masters of the *Ukiyo-e* on my father "Pierre Roche" (recognized by the late Keisuke Niwa, his Japanese friend).

Meditation of a Passerby on His Visit
to the Sacred Woods of Ise
(1959)

> "Just as a thought falls in the mind, as a
> light in the mirror – which is not offended."

To Stephen Yamamoto (Shinjiro)
and to Violet Susman (Mary Agnes)

I

A real "impression," indeed, on my mind, soft and precious, "silky." This visit was short, but so peacefully enjoyed, after the lonely sunset in the sacred wood. At night, in my room, "Futami-kan, No. 19," facing a shallow silent sea, backed by the gentle slope of a hill. And after sunrise on the gulf,[1] the vivid contrast of two, twin colors – light *green* of the square rice-fields, dark velvet *green* of the pine and thuya (hinoki) forest. Both felt as a comfort[2] by the illiterate mind of a foreigner; preserved from enquiring into the meanings of noisy social advertisements, phrases, or scripts. The greens of the landscape acted on me as the *foil* of a mirror of my past, revolving me until my birth-place, strangely found again here. I was no longer a traveler, but a new pilgrim; at rest.

Before leaving France, my eyes had been casually "focused," at dawn, on two kakemonos with spring blossoming trees, kept more than sixty years, from the room of my infancy, where my father had put them. My father was a sculptor under the name

165

of "Pierre Roche"; he had formed his style by studying carefully Greco-Roman and Renaissance artists; he had also been
a student in medicine; and being the grandson of peasants,
ploughmen till the Revolution of 1789, in French Vexin (my
mother's ancestors being weavers in Flanders), he remained per-
meable to the spell of simple agricultural life, to the sense of
a pure mystery hidden behind Nature's naive cruelty. He had
ceased to believe in God, but he confided in the miraculous
birth of France in the fifteenth century, in the virginal apparitions among trees witnessed by Joan of Arc, after her candle
offerings to Our Lady of Bermont in the forest; and he had made
a solitary silent pilgrimage in 1889 to Domremy.[3] The wonder-
fully artistic paradox of inviolated Virginity blessing the tools,
the crops, and harvests, and cattle, was dear to his thought.

Many years after, in 1928, I studied, for a "Livre de Raison"
(family-book) I intended to write for my eldest son, the under-
ground beliefs of the peasants of French Vexin, between river
Oise and river Yerre; and I found Joan of Arc was only one out
of hundreds of similar cases of "devoted" young girls, "Daughters of the Parochial Vow" at May, temporary "priestesses" of
local Virgin's apparitions (as Benoite at the Laus, Amice at Léon,
Bernadette at Lourdes, A. K. Emmerick at Dülmen, Mélanie
at La Salette, Lucia at Fatima). Not precisely the Jewish Virgin-
Mother of conscious Christendom, but her prototype, the immemorial Witnessing Virgin of Transcendency—foreseen, as a
common archetype, from the Greek cave of Persephone (Eleu-
sinian mysteries), to the Japanese cave of Amaterasu-Omikami.
The Virgin with a *Mirror* (not of masculine sexuality, but of
surrendered ecstasy), and a *Sword* (not of masculine sexuality,
but of angelical nakedness), all sparkling fire, as in Joan of Arc.

It was in May 1890, when visiting the first orderly exhibition of Japanese prints in Paris at the Beaux Arts that Pierre
Roche received the shock of the "revelation of Japanese Art":
plunging views, on instantaneous gestures, "pure and simple
observation, from which beauty necessarily proceeds, by some
admirable and unavoidable convenience. The matter of these
prints, in itself, the Japanese paper, inspired in him a kind of

reverence—as in Shinto worship, the *gohei;* it was for him the medium of "purifying" his molded sculptural reliefs. He invented molding in this "flexible" and twistable matter, preciously colored as ivory. Since 1891 seizing with a new sharp outlined style, the life of our country flowers and insects, landscapes and folktales, he created several "modeled prints" which he named "gypsographies," because he printed and colored them on plaster, by his own hand, in single proofs. His friend Keisuke Niwa, the Japanese art critic, drew attention to this new technic, close to that of *sourimonos.* Thirty years later, in 1922, the very year of my father's death, some were shown, and purchased, at the Tokyo exhibition. And in 1935, when the catalogue of his "Estampes modelées et églomisations" was printed in Paris, I sent three copies to Japan, to my friend Dr. V. Bunkei Totsuka (died '39): to have two of them kept in museums.

II

These recollections of my childhood appear now as the cornerstone of my present psychological reconstruction. But for years, these legendary aspects of the traditional culture of peasantry were left behind by this skeptical "grown-up" as mere artistic fancies, superstitions, at my "weaning" from the milk of parental kindness.

Studying, after Sanskrit (and the inscriptions of Angkor), Arabic, and the Moslem countries, traveling for years on the boundaries of the Arab desert in Africa and in Asia, fighting many manlike struggles, I was suddenly struck by the lightning of revelation; disguised, taken prisoner on the frontier of the desert and the rice fields, in Iraq, I could not get rid of this midday sunstroke as I had done with the reflected dawn light-glances of ancestral folktales. Furthermore, these folktales were reanimated in my memory, when I discovered in Islam religious symbols akin to the traditional culture of peasantry. [Among these folk symbols found] in the Islam of monsoon countries, from frankincense Arabia to spicy Indonesia, were the following: those observed in the sky of the annual rising of the Pleiades (in the "Taurus" at sunset, which corrected the primitive calendar of the rice civilization); those beliefs in the preordination of the virginal woman (named either "Mary" or "Fatima," mentioned in the Javanese "Serat Tjentini"), who emanated from the Five First Beings, appearing before Adam and Eve's eyes in the sky of Paradise, as the Star of Predestination, the Guide of the Elect.

I do think that these symbols, before Islamization, had formed already the main tenets of primitive peoples, in the whole rice civilization's area (and also the maize civilization's area).

If the "Goddess Mother of the Rice" is not a virgin in India (Annapurna), she is a virgin in Indonesia: among Bataks (Sumatra) and among Kayan Dayaks of Sarawak (Borneo), whose virgin-priestesses dancing with swords, to hunt and chase bad spirits (without any debased sex-appeal), reminded me of the Shinto rites performed in Ise.

Here and there, we were at the bottom reached by the sounding-line of folklorism; these items were not borrowed, but represented the earliest archetypes of humanity, faith and hope in miracles liberating from determinism, *anterior* to any standardized idol worship, antediluvian promise, from Paradise.

I found perhaps the most suggestive instance of these Shinto-Moslem correspondences in the following theme: the Mirror of the Betrothed, still used in Persia, Afghanistan, and Pakistan for blessing the first encounter between the bridegroom and the spouse. The mirror is hung on the back wall of the hall of meeting; the two have to enter by two opposed doors, and instead of looking straight at each other, they must look askance, at the mirror. Doing so they meet as in Paradise, seeing their faces "redressed" (the right eye at right), not "inverted," as in this world. This mirror is named "Ayine-i-Bibi Maryam," Mirror of Our Lady Mary," probably because it is the "redressed" vision she enjoyed, as primeval virgin, before the creation of bodies, seeing all the Elect, from inside the heart of her shadow-body, in God's own Word.

And it induces me to suppose that, if Amaterasu-Omikami's

mirror found its final resting place in Ise's Inner Shrine, it is because of such a "redressing" glance thrown in the Yatanoka-gami by the priestess, appointed by Suinin, the eleventh emperor. After having crossed, at the holy *"tirtha,"* the Isuzugawa (on the Ojibashi), she may have put the mirror on a tree at her left, to perform her purification on the riverside. Then, rising again, she peeped at the mirror from behind her, at the mirror's *image* reflected on the surface of the water. So her first purified glance could welcome and conceive the ray of light coming from the mirror behind her—this ray, definitely "redressed," giving her the first greeting at her entrance to the Abode of Peace; there to keep the primitive Fire (in the Imibi-yaden, not far behind).

III

I have attempted above to show the "stuff" of my actual understanding of Ise as a religious asylum was slowly and subconsciously woven, as of a chrysalid; the series of threads of my shy vows being crossed, not without pain and anguish, by the warp of destiny. I am still holding on, for the sake of my fathers and countrymen.

Such a notion of pilgrimage looks, to outside observers, as a rather unreal and unfinished escape, a rather paradoxical attempt to jump out of the rationalized human condition of thraldom, of helpless slavery that is not only social pressure, trade, or salary, but also merciless laws of nature, time and space, and axiomatics; in sum, the awful prison "in expansion" of the nebulae. This is the "hope against hope" of a miracle appearing in the center of the universe, which could change our hyperextension through an involution, and unite us as freedmen of a Hidden Guest, half-veiled as before dawn.

Such a notion of pilgrimage, however, is already felt and tasted, for interior sufferers, as the threshold of rescue. We foresee that most of the pilgrims on the path flock together, on lines spiritually converging. Marked out by "subjective" monitions that

are transhistoric, transspatial, and transfinite; that is, by striking premonitions and recalls.

Parapsychological researches have elaborated now, in universities, methods of analysis, so as to ascertain, critically and sta-
tistically, thousands of subjective warnings of this kind, and
establish their validity.

Investigations should be made among the millions of Japanese pilgrims who have visited Ise, since the defeat of the Mongol fleet in the thirteenth century, to discover personal records
of their "spiritual itinerary" to Ise, to learn how their vows had
been answered.

May I suggest that Professor Kunihei Wada's inquiry, on the
behalf of the Konan University in Kobe, could provoke the creation of a Shinto Psychological Bureau of Enquiry at Ise, for the
research of documents, among Japanese pilgrims, of the "spiritual answers" to their vows there.

As a non-Japanese, I have tried above to fetch in my memory,
most minutely, all the subjective and objective elements of a
"prehistory" of my own personal "itinerary" to Ise.

And I submit this humble report to the historians of religions,
with all my apologies for the "egocentric way" unavoidable in
such "psychological investigations," and for the apparent insig-
nificance of this collection of queer instances. One day, perhaps,
they may recognize in Ise one of these National abodes of peace,
on earth, that are, as Jerusalem, as Benares, becoming supra-
national among men, where the right of asylum is supreme, for
all those liable to be summoned at the doomsday of truth, at
the very end.

IV

What answer did I receive personally, and what is the vow,
which being hearkened to, convinced me?

As I have said before, it was slowly, gradually, that all this
indirect information, from my parents in France, and from my
friends in Islam, was understood by my mind, and got "concate-

nated" in my memory. But they became "cogent," and imperative, interfering solemnly with my external life, lately: through
the twofold medium of unwonted "warnings" (in French: "inter-
signes") from outside.

In 1956, the invitation from my Japanese colleagues to the
nineteenth C.I.H.R. in Tokyo, and its intricate realization, August 1958, gradually "reanimated" in me a feeling of personal
inadequacy to my filial duty concerning Pierre Roche's "japaniz-
ing" works, "gypsographies and eglomisations," and their diffu-
sion among experts in Japan, since 1935.

Early in summer, this very year, it was granted to me, unexpectedly, to fulfill a humble spiritual legacy of "reparation"
entrusted thirty-seven years ago in Paris, June 9, 1921, by a Japanese guest of France, R. Adm. Y. Sh.; to three friends of his
first French confidant (Daniel Fontaine), Paul Claudel, Vladi-
mir Ghika, and myself: left alone alive to perform the will. My
acceptance of such a "covenant of friendship" relied on his dis-
closing the secret reason of his legacy of "reparation"; his compunction, for lack of filial piety, toward his father on the day
of his death (1917), when unable to perform for him the traditional tribute of prayer.

The importance of our "covenant" was deepened for me, when,
six months later (January 18, 1922), I had to endure the same
heart-thrilling sorrow.

And nine months after, it was decisively sealed in my heart
when I was designated as "respondent," before the Parisian police, of a foreign girl,[4] sick, suffering, and sacralized to the
"holy souls of Japan" by a vow: a rare and radiant maiden, who
had "guessed" our common secret of filial compunction, "sub-
limating" and healing it by her compassion. She later founded
in Tokyo, with Dr. V. Bunkei Totsuka, a dispensary and a hospi-
tal, nursing and cheering the desperate in the slums.

Exiled from her true country, she died eight years later (February 20, 1950), but the ever-virginal desire of her love still
breathes there; it attracted me as a magnet over the seas, from
her tomb in Dover to the burial place of our Japanese friend
(d. February 20, 1941), at Aoyama Boshi, last August 30.

After all, the only Miracle humanity is longing after, is "Ewig weibliches," as Goethe foresaw, but in the sense of inviolable virginity begetting us to life. It is the earliest miracle in predestination, and the latest in revelation; the final promotion of woman, the first "conception," stainless, of this feeble sex lifting us upwards, setting us ablaze, ending, as Amaterasu Omikami's hidden mirror, by the fire of the burning bush.

For the sake of Japanese friendship, my pilgrim-night in Ise was lived and nearly "danced," liturgically, with the awful sword of hope, by an old lonely mind overflowing with shyness, like the Shirabyoshi's in Lafcadio Hearn's tale.

NOTES

1. Before the Fuji (invisible), a little at my left.

2. *Green* is one of the two colors preferred by Goethe in his psychological classification of colors (Farbentheorie): *green* comforting our senses, *purple* exalting our spiritual dignity.

3. No. 7 of his "eglomisations" (on mica) on this Joan of Arc (1896), was on his studio's table, always. Cf. his "N.D. de Chartres" for Huysmans.

[4. Violet Susman.]

The Temptation of the Ascetic Çuka by the Apsara Rambha

(1961)

The classical tradition of Sanskrit literature has transmitted to us several well-known examples of the theme of the temptress apsara being sent to the gods to force an ascetic to lose the merits of his penance which threatens to overturn the Indian Olympus.

In Sanskrit these narratives describe the encounter of the perfect vow of chastity of the "Brahmachari" with sexual lure. The ascetic can be beaten in this duel which his Promethean attitude has provoked and in which his very identity as characterized by his vow is at risk. The apsara, for her part, obeys the order of the gods with equal risk to her feminine nature. She also can be defeated, and her defeat can be sealed with physical punishment (as in the case of Rambha "petrified" by the curse of Visvamitra). But no Sanskrit text shows us at the conclusion of these duels any positive spiritual result, whether in terms of interchange or genuine relationship, or realization of the need to love that each has or the need to be "objet reflété et valable, en rapport avec le sujet qu'il est" (to quote the profound words of J. J. Mayoux on the heroine of Joseph Conrad's *Victory*).

But in the dialectal languages of modern India, the "vernaculars," from Marathi to Gujrati, from Punjabi to Bengali and Tamil, we find that the oral devotion of illiterate peoples has slowly deepened the Sanskrit narratives of temptation, to the point of *exalting* the incitement to sin scene with grace, *bhakti*, with a

173

spiritual transfiguration that binds and elevates together the ascetic and the apsara.

Popular devotion has chosen to retain only one borderline case of this temptation: pitting the most unshakable of the Brahmacharis, Çukadeo, son of Vyasa, against the most radiant of the apsaras, Rambha, daughter of Kuvera. Already, in the Sanskrit text of the *Mahabharata,* in chapter 333 which describes the supreme flight of the ascetic Çuka, the most beautiful of the apsaras are drawn to contemplate him and their admiration keeps them from any desire to tempt him. But the serene spiritual encounter between them and him stops there; there is no catalysis. In the modern popular meditation, however, particularly in the Marathi dialect, the irradiant splendor of the ascetic Çuka, the naked reality of his chaste youth fills Rambha with astonishment and makes her aware of her "virginally" maternal calling to Çuka.

One can compare a lithograph "made in Germany" with the Marathi text written in versified Davanagari characters. The lithograph was taken from an original painting made for commercial devotional propaganda purposes in 1927 by a Gujrati Brahmin artist, Vasudeo Hiralal Pandya (born in 1895 at Harsol, near Ahmedabad, where he lives in retirement), a member of the Nagar Brahmin caste of Vasalnagar, Vaishnava. The text reproduces page 33 of the *Rambha-Çuka Samvad* (= dialogue of R. and Ç.), versified in the beginning of the seventeenth century by the Marathi poet Mukteshvar, whose lines 7–18 depict the apsara Rambha defending herself against the accusing ascetic who is denouncing her carnal provocations by "opening her heart" to make him smell the perfume of her purity.

An account will be published in *France-Asie* of Tokyo of my chance discovery of this German lithograph in a pagoda in Saigon along with the identification of the "vernacular" text by Mukteshvar. Two close friends of Gandhi and of Brahmacharism, Pyarelal and K. S. Kalelkar, put me on the track. M. J. H. Lakhani (Chhotu) of Bombay was able to locate the address of the painter Vasudeo H. Pandya and to get me the Marathi text of Mukteshvar (and of Uddhava Chighana); this text was analyzed for me in English in Paris by M. Vasant Ambekar, who had heard it recounted by his mother when he was a child in Poona.

Lines 7–18 of Mukteshvar's poem affirmed what the German reproduction suggested initially, not to me alone but also to Pyarelal, in the *prise de regard* between the ascetic and the apsara. It is not a hostile glance between them, not steady and "closed," but an "open" look of mutual "ecstasy," in which the dazzling ascent of Çuka toward the heaven of asceticism enables the beautiful Rambha to "rediscover" her destiny and the end of her role as an apsara: born of the churning of the sea, given of the *amrta*, of the ambrosia which intoxicates with sanctifying immortality, no longer a corruptress born of a flesh doomed to putrefaction but the soul of an Aeschylean Oceanid who consoles a hero coveted by gods.

There is more: in this popular transformation of a classical theme of temptation, the devotion of the humble leads, of itself, without failing to see in it an external influence either from Persian Islam or Syro-Malabrian Christianity, toward a correct solution of the two main religious problems which have troubled the thought of India for so long: that of the number of reincarnations, and that of the unicity of divine truth.

As for the first problem, Çuka says definitely to Rambha, after having scolded her harshly for being a courtesan, that he is ashamed at having doubted the purity of her heart, and for having "withdrawn" from her into the sterile fortress of his asceticism: "forgive me . . . I promise you, when I am born again it will be in your womb [literally, ovary] where I shall have, with all my gratitude, the joy of your pure heart and smell the musk as my lot. And you will be my mother, and I shall have the unique honor of having such a mother as you. I no longer concern myself with my past. What I rejoice in now is the thought that I shall have the privilege of being your son in my new birth." Rambha, upon hearing these words of Çuka, is thrilled, her eyes become filled with tears (of reverence), and she is unable to speak (immediately). There is no indefinite number of rebirths, only the one in which one "reenters the womb of his mother," as Jesus tells Nicodemus.

As for the second problem, Çuka also says definitely to Ram-

bha, who incites him to interrupt his asceticism in order to taste
the joys of Olympus, that he does not want any of that idolatry
which unduly polytheizes divine attributes by individualizing
them (as in the temples of Benares). He rejects their falseness.
Like a true Brahmachari, Çuka has become "one," as Brahman
the atman of the Upanishads, with whom he is joined, is one.
But the perfect ascesis does not end in a simple destruction of
the flesh at the sight of a purely spiritual paradise, any more
than does the heroic *sati* of the faithful widow on the pyre of
her husband. To complete the dialogue between the lover and
the beloved, which pits masculine splendor against feminine
grace in a duel which could only end in mutual destruction,
there is a third interlocutor who effects the joining: love, the
spirit of truth, *satya*, which shatters the "otherness" between
the two and transfigures and resuscitates them "together" in a
sacred place.

Let's look first at the painting, which reflects the rather British academicism that M. Vasudeo H. Pandya had learned in the
studio of Manilal Jani and scrupulously adheres to in the traditional features associated with the theme. Çuka is seated with
naked torso in padmasana (lotus position) on his tiger skin. He
wears the double sivaite rosary, the *mala*, with the sacred cord,
upavita. Rambha, with her two robes, one tight-fitting, the other
loose (half hiding her feet), her headband, and her three brace-
lets on her wrists, stands a little in the background, barely touch-
ing the ground. She is surrounded by all the marvels of spring,
by foliage shaken by the breeze, by flowers opening to diffuse
their scent, by buzzing bees. Water cascades down snow-covered
peaks, either Himalaya or Meru (Lake Anavatapta) from the
Ganga, as from the Neak Pean of Angkor, to bring healing to
bodies and to souls. The exchange of glances glistens transvers-
ally, penetrating the whole landscape with a chaste spiritual
illumination.

Then, the text of Mukteshvar. His stanzas had at first followed literally the original Sanskrit models, keeping the strict
opposition between the unshakeable vow of the ascetic and the
repeated lures of the temptress to carnal joys, along with the

full moon and the intoxication of spring. Certain Sanskrit prototypes follow the antithesis. Mukteshvar, on the other hand (followed by Uddhava Chighana in his *Çuka-Rambha Samvad* from
the end of the seventeenth century) introduces the cathartic
peripeteia. Çuka, in this instance, passes from a general criticism of the carnal hypocrisy of women to its direct application
to his temptress Rambha; and Rambha passes from a general
appeal to sexual pleasures to her personal justification and re-
plies "full of offended pride" by "partly opening her heart," which
confuses Çuka. Overreaching his ascetic steadfastness, Çuka
discovers the pure mystery of the "radiant" beauty of women.

This is what struck me looking at the lithograph in Saigon,
this call to a spiritual exaltation, in a Brahmachari, as Pyarelal
later confirmed for me. India was offering me a solution to the
problem confronting me for many years in an ambiguous form
in Greek and Celtic Christianity—the *syneisaktism* of the agape-
tae of Ephesus and of their "virgines subintroductae," and that
of the pilgrimages of Erin where the beautiful nun Crinog did
not hesitate to "sleep under the same cloak" as a young male
companion in order to make him overcome the temptation she
offered him. Kuno Meyer studied this perilous psychology [Sitzb.
Pr. AK. (Berlin, 1908), pp. 362–374; cf. *Études Carmélitaines*
(Paris, 1951), p. 98, n. 1], in which I readily see the cause for
the failure of the profane syneisaktism attempted together by
Tristan and Iseult.

The Indian solution of the *Çuka-Rambha Samvad* is more
frank: the consummate Brahmachari is assailable, his soul seems
"to be one with peace itself," according to the saying of St. John
of the Cross repeated by Gandhi.

Parallel to the Indian theme of the *apsara who becomes the
mother* of the one whom she risked desiring carnally *at the moment when she makes him inhale the perfume of her heart* by opening it to him, folklore offers us the theme of the *milk springing
from the breasts of a virgin in order to have her become the mother
of a hero* whom she risked desiring carnally. It is the theme
found in Javanese (Raden Pakou) and Indian legends (of Vaisali)
studied by E. Cosquin [*Etudes folkloriques* (Paris, 1922), pp.

199–264, with commentary by Geneviève Massignon, the author's daughter]. These legends are not simple "explanations" of rites of adoption, as René Basset thought; rather they depict the creation of a sanctifying bond of maternity, communal in nature, between the hero and the virgin who uncovers her breast to him (to suckle him) or her heart (for him to smell the perfume of sanctity). It is the theme of the legends of St. Brigid and of St. Germaine; it is the ecstasy of Gertrude van Oosten and of St. Lydwine of Schiedam, who were allowed to nurse the newborn child on the night of the Theophany [J. K. Huysmans, *Sainte Lydwine* (Paris, 1901), p. 242]. The theme repeated by Claudel in his "Violaine," who gave miraculous milk to the child of her bad sister, which caused a sudden cure. [See Richard Griffiths, "Claudel et Sainte Lydwine," in *Bull. Soc. Amis de J. K. Huysmans* (Paris, 1959), no. 387, pp. 436–439.]

It is the evocation of that "milk of human kindness" for which the world thirsts. And if I risk evoking it here today, it is because in our cynical time in which we have seen soldiers finishing off their own wounded on the battlefield to "lighten their burdens" during their movement of troops, the International Red Cross of Geneva (where C. J. Burckhardt lives) is practically the only organization that gives to the wounded, prisoners, and refugees of both enemy camps of today this "milk of mercy." This is why God allowed me, on a certain twenty-second day of March 1956, that I shall never forget, to help Him show in some of the "camps" in Algeria this maternal smile of compassion, "raining" its sweetness on the just and the unjust impartially, on a lacerated humanity which dies when it is cut off from this milk.